BOUQUET FRESH

Hospital Housekeeping with Patient Focus

MARK ROBERTS

ISBN 10: 1479207047

EAN 13: 9781479207046

Library of Congress Control Number: [ENTER NUMBER]
CreateSpace, North Charleston, SC

To the housekeepers ...
for your hard work

I remember a saying once.

It said that if truck drivers do not go to work, if they just decide to sit down and not show up for work, and the trucks stop rolling, everything around the United States would come to a standstill.

Everything would stop.

No Wal-Mart merchandise, no gasoline, no groceries.

Sick people could not get the supplies they need.

No toys for children, no hardware for builders, no new cars.

Without the truckers, we would surely be in trouble.

In light of that thought, think of what may happen if all the housekeepers did not go to work. Everything still running, right? Nothing shuts down; you can still get all goods and services, no problems.

Well, this is correct.

For about a week. Maybe a month.

Then, a few people may start calling 911.

We have to remember that housekeeping is directly in the path of microorganisms that want to take over the world.

Infection control is the part played by housekeepers.

When no cleaning gets done, we can sit back and watch a movie about the Black Plague of Europe – which scientists are still trying to figure out what happened there.

For sure what did not happen was a robust cleaning schedule with housekeepers hired to use brushes, mops, cleaners, disinfectants to stop the scourge.

If they would have had that, perhaps it may have been called the "Black Sickness that was stopped" in which relatively few people were affected.

We will never know, but it is possible the outcome would have been much different with the cleaning knowledge and products we use today.

And now for this book.

Purpose – to see and understand the importance of work done by these housekeepers, and to help supervisors and other people that may have had the same problems I came across.

If the humanity nature of the work is not quite enough of a lure to interest readers, inside the book we'll take a brief mention of two innovators and how this simple concept called housekeeping helped lead them to success, to the top.

One was named Ray Kroc. The second: J.W. Marriott.

EXECUTIVE HOST

YOUR ENVIRONMENT

1. Who Is The Host

When customers visit your hospital/building, who is it that takes the role of host? Perhaps, if your building is an upscale apartment building, a doorman is there to greet them, then an elevator operator.

Or perhaps you personally are waiting at the entrance to give them a warm greeting, welcoming them to your establishment.

If not, in the absence of a greeting personally from you or someone else, the greeting then comes to the guest in the form of a non-person.

The guest looks around, and square in front of their eyes is your building.

Your building becomes the greeter.

If you are shaking hands with the guest, giving them a smile, the guest can feel the warmth of a personal human touch.

Without a human touch, the building is now the thing that touches the guest, and either gives them a warm feeling, or a signal that this establishment is cold and not very friendly.

Your environment is your greeter, and establishes the mood, tone, feelings for the guest before you even get a chance to say "may I help you".

Sam Walton placed a greeter in every store to help with security, but he found that it also helped set the mood for shoppers, that a live person actually greeted them instead of a building.

It seemed to help his business.

In the absence of a greeter, what actions could be taken that would make your building say to the guest –"you are welcome here".

Your environment is your host/greeter.

2. 4 words that brought on case studies

"If I had a brick for every time I've repeated the phrase **Quality, Service, Cleanliness, and Value,** *I think I'd probably be able to bridge the Atlantic Ocean with them."*

– Ray Kroc, founder, McDonalds Corp.

McDonalds, one of the premiere companies in the world, names four main focus points that drive their business. One of the four things is cleanliness. Ray Kroc thought cleanliness so important that it ranked at the very top. He focused on it. Even right before his death, he was known to call the manager of the local McDonalds close to his home and tell him the parking lot had trash to be swept up.

Yet, the cleanliness issue is too often overlooked by many businesses – it's just an item that, while they feel it is somewhat important, the real focus should be elsewhere. After all, they summarize, cleanliness alone cannot pay the bills.

I would agree with this argument, except the nagging thing, if it's not that important, how is it that service businesses, the ones that have paid extraordinary attention to cleanliness, seem to have more success than others?

But, a company literally in the public eye, like a hospital, restaurant, or any public place; would be wise to make these places attractive.

The level of how attractive may sway customers your way, or push them away.

Your environment is host to the customer.

If the host has an ink stain on his tuxedo, what good is that?

The customer frowns and turns around.

Ray Kroc had 4 words. Cleanliness was at the top.

3. Hotel/Hospital Hospitality

Definition of hospitality in the Oxford American Dictionary: *friendly and generous reception and entertainment of guests*

The level at which hospitality is offered could be thought of as not just a cost, but the value placed on friendly and generous receptions.

Most businesses want to be hospitable towards their customers.

Hotels spend a great deal of energy focusing on hospitality; it is in their basic makeup – it is who they are and what they do.

Generally, cleanliness of the environment is lumped into the hospitality definition.

A hotel would not be thought of as being very hospitable while neglecting to provide a clean environment.

In a hospital, many things are like a hotel experience.

Patients are healing, recovering, seeking treatment, but also – sleeping, going to the bathroom, watching TV, taking showers; many things here seem hotel-ish like.

A hospital patient, while going through part healing and part hotel type actions, look around for the hospitality they've come to expect from hotels.

People that have been patients in a hospital will be able to recall if the room appeared clean.

Some of them may be contacted by a third party surveyor.

These turn into your patient satisfaction scores.

The new link between Value Based Purchasing (VBP) and these scores make cleanliness even more important.

Let us attempt to raise those scores.

4. We're Not Doing That Good

Why are many of our hotels cleaner than our hospitals?

Shouldn't our hospitals be the most uncompromising bastion of cleanliness, disinfected with only the best products?

It's true that hospitals are responsible for a more complex job in cleaning than in a hotel.

But the question hospitals struggle with is this:

Why do many of our patients believe we are not doing a good job?

The research is limited, but the cleanliness of a hospital is no doubt one of the contributing factors.

How can we improve.

5. A Study By A Nation

In 1997, the English government launched an ambitious program to improve the quality of health care.

The NHS (National Health System) is the government run hospital system.

It is the largest publicly funded health service in the world, employing 1.7 million people.

As some years went by, the government hired research studies done by different research businesses.

They wanted real reports from real patients on their experiences in the hospitals.

Results came from hundreds of thousands of patients on a nationwide basis.

One finding: Researchers found that cleanliness was a top item when patients were deciding where to have treatment – in fact it ranked near the top.

A little more research would not hurt.

6. Cleanliness Trumps Free Food

From the book "*Trump University Marketing 101*", a survey was cited.

The survey asked customers to rank 19 different casino and service attributes in order of importance.

Customers top priority was not free rooms, free food, or other amenities.

The attribute most important to loyal customers was cleanliness.

The customers preferred a clean building over free food.

For them, food is easier to obtain than clean surroundings.

They wanted to be able to use their slot machines, play their games without worrying about whether, after they had spent a considerable amount of money in this casino, they would find urine on the toilet seats at the next break.

The casino's food selection is amazing. Is the cleanliness also amazing?

Clean is difficult to produce and hard to find.

Do the difficult.

7. Forty Years of Research

"There is an intractable connection between high levels of customer satisfaction and increased shareholder value".

JAMES D. POWER IV OF J.D. POWER AND
ASSOCIATES

In his book, "Satisfaction", James Power outlines the connection between higher customer satisfaction with higher shareholder value, higher profits.

Time and again, the proof is there; his data is factual and hard to dispute.

From retail businesses, to car manufacturers, the result is the same: the higher the satisfaction, the higher the customer loyalty.

Another thing he mentioned: the application even applies to public utilities that enjoy a near monopoly in the area they serve, because it's cheaper to not have to address the same customer problems time and again.

Some hospitals have a near monopoly in their area – it would simply be cheaper to increase satisfaction anyway.

If customer satisfaction increases loyalty, and the number one request from customers is a spotless building – the conclusion could be that housekeeping may be far more important than some ever imagined.

J.D. Powers has more than forty years of research experience.

The facts of his research are hard to dispute.

8. "Not A Revenue Producing Source"

How many times this phrase has been uttered by managers, about why housekeeping should take lower consideration in hospitals/businesses; the phrase needs to be put to rest now.

If you own a service, especially a service where people are sleeping in a room, ordering food, using your restrooms, observing your uniforms – the effort should be to make every front and back of the house area as crystal clean as possible.

It's expensive.

Something more expensive – losing a customer.

Your appearance must be stellar, or revenue may be lost. Forever.

9. Steering on A Different Track

People are not sure why it's so difficult to provide a clean building, a clean hospital.

A few things to think about:

Administering medicine in today's times, has become so fraught with technicalities, that if it were a football game, the game would never be played because the players would have to graduate a doctorate in football, then deal with government regulations on how to throw a forward pass. If the pass is not thrown correctly, litigation concerns come up, even prison penalties.

Since nobody wants this, all the effort is placed into getting the things right that government and state regulations say must be done to avoid these unpleasant things.

Understandably, over the last several decades, hospitals have had to turn their attention to the major issues of medicine – which are enormous.

Cleaning began to slip in some quarters as years went by.

Then, in came the professionals.

10. The Pro's and Con's

Hospitals had to focus on medicine, and were distracted from administering the technical aspects of thousands of decisions and thousands of employees, that when the call was made from housekeeping for attention, the administers were spent – worn out.

The new technologies these administers had to deal with were so advanced and the decisions had to be so thought out and handled correctly, that it outstripped the ability, of many of these fine men and women, to spend precious time on housekeeping decisions.

Not knowing for sure how to measure what it should cost to clean their building, and not having the energy to waste time; they outsourced it to the bid process.

There were so many custodial contractor salesmen that came by and promised so many things and failed to meet promises in many instances.... that some hospitals became lost and found few they could trust.

Some contractors were shown the door. Some were awarded contracts.

Administrations had an extremely difficult time.

The administers tried their best, but were let down by some cleaning companies.

Service with a smile? Confusion reigned, with more frowns than smiles.

Hospital cleaning is simple, but not easy. And expensive.

CLEANING BEGINS
WITH PEOPLE

11. The Vision To Invest

"Your vision will become clear, only when you can look into your own heart"

– CARL JUNG

Many books will speak of how your people should be first, but do we invest in them?

Do we spend time training, working with our associates, and does that produce results?

Most would agree that the investment is worth it.

Can you imagine the kind of boss you would like to work for and then become that kind of boss to your people?

What kind of perfect workplace could we dream about, and then act to make it happen. Would it produce better results, or the same?

Can we improve on what currently exists.

It starts with them.

12. Start

The answer to the previous question could be:

Why not – try to produce the workplace that others dream about.

We must do this to survive.

We must push to develop this workplace before even our existence is taken from us, which could very well happen.

Competitors come along.

Regulations everywhere.

Apathy starts among the workers.

Just a boring place to clock in – just another place to collect a check, wait for Friday and hit the road.

Develop now.

To avoid a below average, or average workplace.

Why not reach for the best.

Why not.

13. 8 gigs or 16? Very little has changed.

The information age has had very little effect on what it takes to clean a hospital.

Still takes old fashioned elbow grease.

Dozens of laptops, software, and reports can be of little help to housekeeping in as much as actual, physical work in getting the building clean.

It's a physical business; a laptop can't scrub a building.

It's "boots on the ground", with more physical action required than a drill sergeant could hand out.

Muscles and stamina for the long term are desirable.

It's not a Monday thru Friday 16 week course either; the needs are 24/7.

An athlete in good physical condition would have the stamina to perform well in a housekeeping role.

Since there are very few athletes or NFL linebackers at the peak of their physical career, filling out housekeeping applications, the work is instead performed by a variety of all types of people, from all walks of life.

These good folks feel they have indeed played a football game after the work day is over – housekeeping can leave you with a lot of sore muscles.

Even with the physical need, top customer service skills are also needed.

Manpower, smiling faces; it's an old fashioned recipe.

14. Hiring Customers

Andersen:

> " *Captain redlegs is the worst enemy those men have got. I thought you said regular federal authorities would be in charge here.*

> *Politician: Captain redlegs is the regular federal authority here now.*

> *- FROM THE MOVIE OUTLAW JOSEY WALES*

In the movie, the wrong person was hired for the job.

Captain Redlegs was the wrong choice to be placed in charge.

Hire people that care about people.

Then, work as a "salesman" for the company and turn these new hires into customers.

Your employees are part of your customer base.

You must get them to "buy" into the company, to be sold on the products, sold on the service - but especially YOU.

You work to take care of their every need – just like a customer.

The employees buy it – they buy you.

They're sold on you and in turn will do anything to help you and the company.

In the hiring interview, look for people that give indicators they would be able to "buy in" to your whole deal, because there are some that can't – or won't.

An employee is also a customer.

Dream to Compete

15. Ask Why

Sizing up your position to determine where you are, and where you want to be is the first step.

It may take a gut check to be honest, but these questions are essential:

Are we true competitors?

Are we taking action to outperform our competitor?

Do the customers prefer our hospital/business over our competitor?

Do the competitor's employees wish they were working for us?

Does the competitor wish they were more like us?

If not, why not?

16. Find An Enemy

The people reporting to you need a reason to improve.

Without a reason, they may just pass time looking for the clock.

Some people in your group may like to compete.

Talk about your competitors and how well they're doing.

Let the competitive juices flow.

You will find that a few of your people will respond, and want to know how to be better.

The workers that respond to your call to compete are your true warriors, and they are capable to win battles for you.

Competition is good.

17. No Enemy? OK, It's You Against You

Don't have a competitor in your area?

Compete nationally, or even you against you.

Compare previous data and strive to continually improve.

The key is to place that data up for all to see.

Without a score board, how does the team know how they're doing?

Keep the score board current

18. Setting the Standard

Ross Perot was once asked what he considered an EDS'R; an EDS'R being an employee that worked for his company, Electronic Data Systems.

"A person that will go anywhere, anytime, 24 hours a day, 7 days a week, to make sure we are the finest computer company in the world, and that nobody beats us in competition", replied Perot.

Setting the bar too high?

Your competitor may be planning to raise the bar to the moon.

You have to shoot for the stars.

19. Reduce To The Ridiculous

A whisper about perfectionism – pursuit of it is required to reach top level service. You need to find reasons why you need to provide the absolute most clean environment possible.

When you can finally find the reasons to be turned on to do this, convincing your staff to do the same is not easy.

Here is the problem: if you even so much as find a single human hair in a patient room, that hair must be removed.

If I find a speck or a spot on the wall – I consider that room

"trashed out" until the spot is wiped away. But that's ridiculous.

That's right. Perfectionism is about doing things that other people think is ridiculous.

That is what you look for in inspections, and take care of it.

Possible? You must believe it is.

Perfectionism chasing is not stupid, it is what can set you apart from everybody else.

For your staff, reduce the explanation of the goal to the ridiculous; tell them that even a single hair should be removed when found.

They may not get it at first – but you must lead by example.

You can't ask for, what you are not willing to do yourself.

Details can be ridiculous – and drive performance like no other.

20. Almost Free Today

The young boy stood there, offering handmade cotton hammocks for sale in Acapulco, Mexico. I could tell he needed to make a sale very badly.

His pitch – "Almost Free" he said, trying to convince us he had a good price on those hammocks. I bought one, even though I did not need it.

I've used the experience when purchasing anything.

"Even if it's free", I'll ask myself – do I really need this item?

Will I really wear those shoes or that jacket – even if the thing is free.

If the answer is no, the item is left on the shelf.

How many of your customers may think in the same way.

Even if you offer your service, your medical clinic, your hospital services for free or at a reduced cost; will the customer really want it or need it if they have to enter a dirty building to get it?

Some will say no, and that is a challenge.

Charge a decent price, offer a decent environment.

21. Challenge your own ideas.

"Have you ever noticed, when you're driving; the person going slower than you is an idiot, and the person going faster than you is a maniac".

– GEORGE CARLIN

Sometimes I think that only my way is correct, that everyone else is either an idiot or a maniac, then I remember the Carlin quote.

Continually challenging your beliefs, can lead to a higher understanding, a strengthening of many positions, and an abandonment of things that should be forgotten.

It's what I learned after I thought I knew it all, that counted.

22. Maybe it's a book

Where can motivation come from?

Again, a story about Ross Perot.

Perot said a turning point was when he read a quote in a Readers Digest, that said "the masses of men lead lives of quiet desperation".

Ross did not want to be desperate, so he started his own business which eventually made him wealthy.

A subscription to Readers Digest may not be a bad idea, but your motivation can come from anywhere.

Wherever it comes from, use it to motivate and achieve.

23. Focus

Sam Walton, when writing his book "Made In America", indicated that competing with Walmart may be easier than some think. He gave in his book the example of Gap stores.

Gap can focus and specialize in areas Walmart cannot.

Upscale clothing. Designs and colors.

A niche.

Can you have a niche in cleaning? In a hospital?

A focus is as much about getting something done as it is about motivating the staff.

Select one area and announce that "we will be the best at this, within 100 miles of all hospitals".

For example:

If you want to be the best at keeping your equipment clean, at keeping your wet floor signs spotless – then focus on that task, until you know you're the best within 100 miles.

Does it work?

Today Gap is still there despite Walmart's always low pricing.

They may not have been there, if they had simply followed the same thing Walmart was doing, and tried to match prices.

Likewise, your people can keep their minds engaged, survive, outlast, and be the best at something, if a niche is created and focused on.

It's a confidence builder, to know you are the best.

Be the Champion of a narrow focus, a single item.

24. Release Potential

Albert Einstein, regarding how he came up with the Theory of Relativity, said that

"it was the happiest thought of my life".

He dreamed it up.

There were no bosses, managers, engineers, guys with masters degrees, real smart people, or anybody else to guide Einstein in his finding.

He was a clerk - a postal clerk.

The scientific world was shocked at this nobody clerk.

Who did this guy think he was?

People with imagination are often labeled as not living in the real world.

The real world took notice, when Einstein turned loose the power of his imagination.

Some people shy away from anything new, they want to keep it real.

You can have both: keep it real plus explore options.

Embrace possibilities.

25. Your Turn To Dream

"I don't know the key to success, but the key to failure is trying to please everybody"

– BILL COSBY

The dream for you is a dream of focus.

Trying to please everyone will get little results – just a few people to say 'thank you' along the way.

If you need a direction, focus on the customer.

You will never lose by doing that.

The mark of a great manager is that of visionary.

Not recognition seeking, but a determination for results.

A vision to focus on a single item, and to be the best at that one thing; in fact the best in that category – in the United States.

Or the best in several categories.

People successful at this are usually willing to self-sacrifice in order to achieve the big banana.

That is, to know you've achieved the top spot in the category even if nobody recognizes this fantastic accomplishment.

Non-recognition comes with the territory in some instances. It's part of the deal, but those driven to reach the mountain summit, do it for the sheer joy of doing it. Just do it, Nike says.

Who says you're not smarter, more brainy than the others to achieve this?

Just take and run with it. Recognition may not happen.

Excuse Me, is Someone Cleaning My Room?

26. OK.

So you step into the main entry of a hospital, aesthetics appealing.

Maybe a Starbucks coffee bar off to the side. Nice.

You ask for directions to a destination from the lovely volunteer lady.

You step in the restroom. Not bad.

This is a clean hospital.

In another part of the hospital, an evening house-keeping supervisor gets slammed with rooms.

A lot of admissions on this night.

"Just get this one done fast", he says to the scurrying housekeeper, "then do a stat in 4020".

The housekeeper finishes the room in near record time – about 18 minutes, leaving behind a "clean" patient room.

The room is called to admissions as ready – satisfying the admissions clerk with a patient that's been sitting right in front of her desk for the last hour, waiting for a room.

"We're sorry", the clerk says to patient. "Sometimes housekeeping is a little slow".

Speed is there, but due diligence may be lacking.

27. Behind The Scenes

In another hospital, a skilled housekeeping manager enters a patient room.

She pulls out a cotton swab, and runs it over the bed rail. Another swab, she runs over the phone. Another swab, on the toilet. Each swab is placed in a special holder, then fed into the ATP reader for analysis. Result – readings are too high, well above the goal.

Upon visual inspection, the supervisor also finds a blood spot on the wall, and hair on the bathroom floor. These items were not readily visible to the previous cleaning person – easily missed and that's why this supervisor makes regular checks.

If the supervisor can find a housekeeper, she will have her do a re-clean.

But everyone is busy, and a new patient will be admitted to this room in less than one hour.

The supervisor has a multiple choice option here.
A. Find a housekeeper, quickly.
B. Ask if the patient can wait a while longer.
C. Supervisor must clean herself.
D. Do nothing.

Depending on demands from her superiors, she could choose any option. With extreme areas to cover, though, finding a housekeeper in time is not likely. Asking the patient to wait even longer will bring frowns all around.

She can clean herself, but the phone keeps ringing for immediate needs.

She is a top notch professional, so option C is chosen, and she looks for a disinfectant wiper pack to clean up this room.

Nothing will be left un-done or un-cleaned, for she is a professional.

This hospital has a high performing supervisor, not accepting anything below her high standards.

These are the behind-the-scenes difference makers.

28. No Explanation

In yet another hospital, a supervisor comes across a discharge patient room being cleaned, but the housekeeper is on the floor.

As the supervisor comes in closer, she can see that the housekeeper is wiping the foot support pull out of a recliner chair.

"What are you doing?" says the supervisor.

But the housekeeper can offer no explanation. It's just something she does – she cares for her rooms, and is known to get down low to clean things others may not clean.

She is also known to keep her cart in immaculate condition, with everything kept in organized shape.

She is not known as a person that can explain that well – she is known as a doer.

A person of action.

And almost nobody knew her dedication, save for the supervisor.

The supervisor rewarded her hard working ladies and men with sweets and food she purchased every week for them as a reward.

There was no explanation for that either. She just did it.

29. Football Sunday

You are in charge of housekeeping at several stadiums.

Opening the broom closet at Cowboys stadium in Arlington to get ready for work, you get a call that several people have spilled their drinks at Chiefs stadium in Kansas City.

You are instructed to get on a plane, fly there and clean up within 20 minutes.

Yes, fly from Dallas to Kansas City, clean up the mess in the same time it would take to order a burger.

This scenario is impossible, but an illustration that paints a picture.

The travel time and vast floor space areas, particularly in medium to large hospitals, turns easy tasks into extreme tasks.

It can seem like flying from Dallas to Kansas City, minus the free movie.

Hospitals that are so large, they are like cities – usually with hundreds or thousands of employees, food courts, cafeterias, hundreds of restrooms, and generate enough trash to fill a billionaire's 25-room Miami beach cottage.

Nobody can fly to Kansas City and mop up the stadium all in 20 minutes.

In the same way, nobody can travel through a large hospital in 20 minutes, going to all the patient rooms, offices, restrooms, food stops.

Yet, the job requires quick service within any location of the facility.

To even walk through and visit the entire building may take several hours or even days.

It takes large crews and state of the art communication equipment to run an efficient housekeeping department, both of which may not be found in your local hospital.

The managers need to be in good condition to keep up with the pace.

Support your managers.

30. A Rose Garden needs a Meticulous Gardener

Patients, very sick patients.

Slept in this room. Many times.

Hundreds of times. Hundreds of days.

Sick person after sick person, one after another.

This all occurred in the same room, your room, hundreds of times.

This is your room now.

The logo on the entrance and brochures are delightful.

And a room by any other name will smell just as sweet, or maybe not so.

Many people don't think about this question:

How much time does this facility spend in cleaning?

Cleaning its rooms, or any other area for that matter.

If this were a rose garden, you could tell if the gardener were taking care.

Some managers are like gardeners, taking care of your room like a rose garden.

Some managers can spot a hair on the floor from ten feet away.

Seek a meticulous manager.

Define What it Takes

31. Definition of "clean".

Dictionary definition: free from dirt, marks, pollutants.

Since customers don't have time to go around examining surfaces to see if they fit the dictionary definition, they make snap judgments.

People look over a room for two to three seconds, and make a judgment.

This is called perception.

Discerning folks may take more seconds, or even a minute, but probably come up with the same judgment they would have anyway using only two to three seconds.

"Clean" is what each individual perceives it to be.

One person's perception of clean is a different person's perception of dirty.

Nobody checks a room to see if it meets the dictionary definition.

What they can, and will do, is check a single item, make a quick sweep of the room with the blink of an eye, make a snap judgment, then move on.

"Clean" is decided in a few seconds, and it's a perception.

32. A False Measurement

How much time it takes to clean, means actually how much time it takes to reduce complaints, for many organizations.

With an organization that thinks like this, the litmus test is to count how many complaints come into the office.

Few complaints, in their mind, means they are giving a fantastic performance.

When in fact, most people are too busy in today's hurried times to complain – if they decide you have a dirty building, will just decide that next time, they'd better look around for your competitor.

In most cases, they will not contact you to complain, they'll just move on down the road.

Complaints are a poor way to judge performance.

33. We'll Do It By Spec

I remember making a sales call on a man, years ago that had contract janitorial work at an

Air Force base. He showed me the specification sheets, a massive multiple sheet extreme detail on what he was mandated to clean, how often, with everything to the dotted T.

He just kind of laughed and said that he cleans the Air Force base like any other building in town and pays little attention to these specifications.

Many people have tried to describe in highly detailed specifications, the definition of what cleaning should be in their facility.

Specs can be so detailed that the custodial service can become confused and may go financially under to fulfill them to the actual letter.

Specs are necessary to maintain an agreement – it's better for both sides to understand them before signing anything.

Specs are part of the business, but since they would have to be monitored constantly over vast floor areas to ensure compliance, they are sometimes of little help in the long run to obtain a quality job.

Endeavor to hire people that are determined to do the job even when nobody is looking.

The people can make a difference, where the spec may not.

34. I Can't Get to Motel 6, Much Less Marriott

"Nothing can resist the human will that will stake even its existence on its stated purpose."

– BENJAMIN DISRAELI

It was this quote that helped me long ago to understand what it takes to perform at excellence levels. To be willing to go all in to meet the challenge.

If your cleanliness is leaving you with the feeling that you are in a nasty environment, that this has the feel of a dirty gas station instead of what should be a dust, dirt, germ free hospital with the best fragrances, soaps, paper – just remember that since this annoys you, this is the first step for improvement.

Sometimes it takes somebody to be annoyed about something before anything is done. The next step is to realize that it takes extraordinary dedication to produce a clean facility, that can at least come close to the cleanliness of a nice standard Motel 6.

Motel 6 should not be discounted for the quality they bring to the table in the hospitality industry.

Some hospitals cannot match the visual cleanliness of a Motel 6.

We have to do better.

35. Cleanliness Up, Scores Down

The manager was able to produce cleanliness second to none.

The hospital was a brand new facility.

But the actual scores related to cleanliness from a third party surveyor sank like an anchor chain.

Checking under the hood, it was revealed that communication with customers was lacking.

Yes, that will do.

Cleanliness plus Communication.

J.W. Marriott & the Anticipation Kings

36. Anticipate

The finest waiter does not ask if you tea needs filling.

He/she anticipates.

Your tea is filled automatically.

The waiter/waitress anticipated a need, and performed with asking the customer.

The bread is replenished without asking.

In fact, many things were done without one word of asking from the loyal patron.

The carpet was vacuumed, in anticipation the customer may want a clean carpet.

The table and chairs were wiped down, in anticipation the customer may want clean tables/chairs.

The environment was prepared. The customer did not have to deal with drab wallpaper, ancient history decorations that appeared as if they were purchased at a run down dollar store in 1985, low lighting that perhaps came from the latest vampire movie.

Instead of all this, an astute manager went out and spent a few hundred dollars on some fresh items to surround the customer.

In addition, the menu was brought promptly without asking.

The window shades were opened to let in some sunshine, without asking.

Everything was anticipated.

The customer is pleasantly surprised by this level of service.

When the check arrives, the customer feels moved to leave a larger than normal tip for all these small actions the waiter thought of and gave freely.

You are the customer. You know you'll be back.

Anticipate.

37. Marriott's Observation

" Our competition, as you know, has loaded their places with employees, I have seen as many as eleven people behind the counter and always somebody in front cleaning the tables and keeping the outside clean. It is one of the reasons for their success. Let us not cut down our employees in any of our operations at the expense of sanitation and service". **

– J. WILLARD MARRIOTT

Invaluable lessons from a hotel chain with 2,500 locations worldwide.

Marriott says in this quote that one of the reasons for success was having plenty of people cleaning. He closely watched his competition and strived to outperform them.

Difficult path to follow? Maybe

38. Marriott's Key For Success

J. Willard Marriott, the man that built the hotel chain bearing his name, had a management philosophy on acute attention to small things.

"Some of my remarks may appear to be too detailed, but it's the little things that make the big things possible. The close attention to the fine details of any operation – restaurants, hotels, or what-not – makes that operation first class".**

– J. Willard Marriott

When it comes to cleaning, fine details down to the finest speck of dust, to a single hair; can make a difference between winners and losers.

Marriott understood this.

Overlook nothing.

39. Clean Restrooms

Just for fun, in 2008 I drove around the Dallas/Fort Worth area.

I had an inspection form designed by me, with 16 spot check items – for rendering a score of cleanliness in public restrooms.

Inspected were 500 public restrooms over a 4 month period – hotels, restaurants, retail stores – even gasoline service stations.

Among the hotel chains, Marriott brands outscored competing hotels.

Ritz Carlton is a Marriott brand, and ranked #1 for all categories.

Of the other Marriott brands, Springhill Suites was number 4, and Fairfield came in at number 8 (out of 20 brands and 47 total hotels checked).

Marriott Hotels came in @ #10, and so all four Marriott brands were in the top 10 (out of 20).

The Marriott branded hotels also ranked #1 in what I called my "luxury" category, with the best quality paper and soap available.

2,500 locations worldwide.

Better sanitation, better quality may lead to more locations.

40. A Little Less Conversation . . .

A lot more action.

Elvis's song about satisfaction speaks to the customer/patient.

Many customers may have these thoughts:

"Just take care of my needs for basic stuff like cleanliness, politeness, food, medications. No need for useless talk."

"Tell me what I need to know, but I'd rather have superior action rather than long speeches."

Communication yes, wasting time – no thanks".

It's about effective conversation, not quantity.

If the guest asks for extra talk, that is the time.

Otherwise, Elvis had a good message.

Another anticipation moment.

Bouquet Your Building

41. When the Customer See's Your Building, They See You

The following is an excerpt from the book

"What Clients Love" by Harry Beckwith:

"Every service ultimately sells an experience: the experience of receiving the service. But what is that experience?

We assume that service providers provide that experience by the way they serve their customers; we assume that customer service *is* the experience.

We are half right.

The practical Winston Churchill hinted at the missing half when he observed,

"People shape buildings, then buildings shape people."

Your environment – your building, setting, the entire surroundings of your client's experience – does not merely package you. It changes, and becomes a critical part of, each client's experience."

Beckwith goes on to say this: "Your environment is your client's experience", and the advice is to make your environment exceptional.

Beckwith has been hired by clients such as Microsoft, Target stores, Gillette,

Hewlett Packard, Fidelity Investments – to come and give lectures on improving market share.

Harry Beckwith understands the customer experience

42. I'd like to find a good Mexican Restaurant

You drive into a strange town with your spouse. Must have food.

Chinese, or whatever. So the hunt begins.

One restaurant comes into view, but it's the first one. Keep driving.

Another, then another.

"Honey, we can't find a place".

"That one doesn't look good", you reply.

Here poses the question. How did you base the conclusion?

By the outside appearance. Just did not look like a great place.

Do people choose hospital's like this? Possibly and probably.

Maybe not in an emergency. But for elective surgery....

That's right. You may want to patrol for trash & hire a landscaper – seven days a week if you are open seven days.

People driving by your building right now are forming opinions, and those cars are rolling by 24 hours a day.

Check the outside.

43. When the Customer Knows Your Building, They Know You, At Least A Little Better

When I started my first job in sales at Matera Paper Company in Abilene, TX, the competitors in town were well entrenched, well known as good companies, and we were relatively the new company with an out of town owner. So how do you break through that?

The customers certainly had a hard time taking me seriously. I was 19 years old and obviously green and knew next to nothing about them. I worked hard and they noticed, but for this one exception, what else did I have.

The manager had made up a brochure for us to hand out, and on the front of that brochure was the picture of our building. A few years went by, and I handed out hundreds of these brochures.

I began to notice that, when I gave this brochure to someone I had never met, they would sometimes pause and stare several seconds at the photo on front.

A few of them would say something like "Oh yeah, I know where that is".

I began to catch on. All of a sudden, the focus was changed from "I don't know you", to "I know who you are now". They understood where the building was, and had driven by many times on their way to another place. It clicked in their mind as to where my company conducted business. So when they say "I know your building, that can lead right into "I know a little more about you".

People will ask, "where are you from". They need this information to process a fix on a location.

Geography is something we all believe in. We believe that buildings, parks, streets, post offices are real – that they exist in fact. In today's virtual salesman society, where animated people and companies pop out of phone screens and 3D TV sets almost real-like, but everyone knows it's fake ; the customer may be grappling with how to grab onto something real – like a brick and mortar building.

People want to get hold of a real person on customer service phone inquiries, and they also like real buildings. We may believe more in a real location than a stranger handing us a business card.

By people understanding your location, they may believe more in you.

That is the magic that breaks through, breaks the ice. When the customer says "I know you", or "I know where you are", you've just made a giant leap.

It did help that our building was actually an historic building in Abilene.

At first, I had thought of the building as a dumped out, run down hideous warehouse.

But that building had been around since 1904 and although many did not know the history behind it, the photo of that building made the magic happen because my customers knew where I was, and then they knew me.

This goes to the environment. If they don't know you, they may believe your building, your environment more than they believe you, at least initially.

The environment may be the key to winning the trust you need in a customer, patient, guest, or anyone else.

The environment matters.

44. My Building Is Nothing Special, So What Next

Having an extravagant building like the millionaire's mansion that appeared in last months issue of Architectural Digest magazine is not necessary.

However, spruce up your building and land-scaping as budget affords.

A hospital has everyone from the public coming there 24/7.

They are judging on your ability to do something about your appearance.

And they will judge on the speed in which you do it.

Plans that are for 10 years in the future means that you may have to wait 10 years to attract customers.

Take care of your appearance.

45. Honey, This Hospital Is Clean

The Feb 15, 2012 writing on the UK's telegraph. co.uk, ** had this article headline:

TripAdvisor-style reviews by patients 'predict worst hospitals'

– It said this: A study by Imperial College London found that hospitals with good hospital ratings on the internet tend to have a 5 percent lower death rate and 11 percent lower re-admission rates. This comes from patients rating their hospital on the NHS (UK hospital system) web site -

Further, and perhaps more importantly, the study said that hospitals with the best cleanliness ratings – (ratings by patients) had a 42 percent lower rate of MRSA infections than those rated the dirtiest.

The research is based on more than 10,000 reviews of hospitals on the NHS Choices website.

Internet ratings may be coming your way.

They are already on the Medicare web page (hospitalcompare.hhs.gov), but the public is not so much aware of that site.

The UK made sure the entire nation knew about it.

If it takes hold in the US, your hospital may be set up on a web site like TripAdvisor, will be affixed a score by the public, and it will include a cleanliness rating.

Increasingly, people rely on reviews on the net to shop, find hotels, and now hospitals may be next.

Be prepared for TripHospital

Room Standards

46. Check your Blank Off

Thomas Edison failed thousands of times before the light bulb was invented.

Or you may say that he *checked* a thousand times.

He checked every possibility, till the correct solution was found.

In housekeeping, checking has no end.

As a supervisor, the act of checking should be most of the job.

Constantly following up on every detail.

Checking and checking, till there is nothing left to chance.

And then, doing something about it – immediately.

You may need an ibuprofen, but in the end, mastering this action has a payoff.

You may not invent a light bulb, but you'll invent for yourself a performance like no other.

Let those that understand and can follow this rule, do so.

47. "Bed In The Room" Standard

Unfortunately, a hospital out there may have a simple way to measure when a room is ready for the next patient: There is a bed in the room. That is the gold standard.

Housekeeping cleaned the room, but no further checks were performed.

This is similar to hopping into an Boeing 757 for a flight, and the only check performed by the ground crew was to make sure seats are still available, that the seats have not been removed by anyone, and a cleaning person vacuumed the them off.

Nobody performed a routine check of the mechanical, checked pressure levels, checked anything else – just passenger seats – the plane is ready for take off.

When the plane goes down, people wonder what happened.

The standard must be higher.

48. I'd Rather Explain the Price than Apologize for the Quality

Twenty-five to thirty minutes cleaning time is about the average in hospital patient room cleaning.

In many situations, maybe only twenty minutes.

By comparison, hotels allow at least 20 minutes.

In hotels, the previous occupant was not sick, with the room in need of a deep clean.

As a manager, I constantly have to re-think and allow more time. These rooms must be done well.

Almost good is not good enough.

No Compromise.

49. Nobody Does It Better – Or At All

Checking room conditions for the next patient coming in – you may find nobody does this in your hospital. Nobody in any department.

A nurse may glance around, but that's about it.

The nurse must take care of focusing on the patient medications and reports anyway, so it's you.

It falls to you. You have to do it.

You need a list.

But, as in everything – your checklist will not be ordinary.

You have to be the best in the industry.

Checklists can be boring.

A boring paper may be ignored – you have to get the team to buy into it.

Spice it up.

Dress up your quality checklist.

50. Customer Turnover

You go into Joe's Taco Barn for your breakfast burrito, fat calories be damned.

Hate mail awaits today, you say, so to hell with it.

As your mouth waters for taste of the sausage, you notice that customers are hurried through the line at a breakneck pace, the food is kind of thrown around and not well prepared, and it appears no real quality standards are followed.

The next day, you decide to try another place.

Room Turnover.

A commonly used term that needs a total re-thinking.

It's about quickly getting a room ready for next patient.

Using the word "turnover" can be taken that the hospital is in a hurry and standards may not be met, just like Joe in his Taco Barn fine meal establishment.

"Room preparation" is a much more pleasant term, and is a creative term – you are creating a prepared room without dictating that speed is the only measured criteria. You are preparing a room just like a chef prepares a delicious dish.

Room preparation could be one of the most critical points in customer retention in a hospital, a hotel, or wherever a person spends the night in a room.

If it can be done quickly, this is preferred. Too quickly, and problems turn up.

How the hospital handles room preparation can mean the difference between that customer coming back, or waltzing over to a competitor next trip.

The times that I hit my highest customer satisfaction, I will quickly attribute to two things: room preparation, and the total dedication of my loyal, hard working and deserving housekeeping staff.

In order to prepare those rooms, many times found myself bargaining for more time on the room with nursing staff, which they are generous in giving.

For me, it felt like a war because of the physical demands, time demanded, and the price paid for excellence.

Re-think

51. In Some Cases, Stat Fast Is Not Good

If no checks are done and the room is prepared without due diligence, the guest becomes the person that must, in a de facto way, become their own inspectors.

This cannot happen.

They could come across things that no excuse can be given.

If it happens, then the cleaning that should have been done in the first place, must be done in front of guests or the guest must be offered another room.

The mantra here must be – no way, and never.

Inspect.

52. "No Matter What" Promise

"I will make a covenant of peace with them"

– EZEKIEL 37:26

The entire Bible seems to be built on a single principle – the promise.

The promise referred to would be an everlasting promise, a "no matter what" promise that will stand the test.

Should we be making promises to customers?

Perhaps.

It can be the most powerful thing of all.

In business, the time a promise flexes its muscle is when the temptation comes to break it, but instead the promise remains faithful to the customer.

And it's not a policy that comes under temptation and remains faithful, but rather a single employee that makes this decision.

A loyal employee that is willing to possibly endure some discomfort and maybe even hardship in order to uphold a promise made by the company to its customers.

Something extraordinary – an individual that makes a promise to themselves to uphold the highest standards even when the company believes such service may be too difficult for the individual to bear.

"She will still be smiling to our guests after 12 hours on her feet?"

"She can't handle it", but in fact she does.

The honor should go out to this worthy employee.

Businesses make promises but individuals keep them.

Reward them for the promise kept.

53. Keep it.

How can the principle of promise fit in with business.

I think it means this: keep a promise and keep a customer.

If you have a business, you are making at least an insinuated promise.

That is, to do what your brochure/commercial/ yellow page ad, says you will do.

Customers have basic expectations and want basic service.

Breaking the expectation is breaking the promise they thought you were making.

Expectation not met/Promise not met.

Customers have an uncanny ability to know if you are meeting expectations.

Keep the expectation/keep the promise/
Keep the customer.

54. Forever.

Do you have to keep a promise forever?

No.

For honor, yes.

A person/business can sometimes break an expectation/promise.

The service can be lowered to save money.

Customers may not notice.

When they notice, will they overlook?

Maybe.

But not for long.

An average business with average service does this.

Some businesses view honor like they view perfection – unachievable and unprofitable.

So they don't try.

Try.

55. Would you recommend this hospital?

This question on your survey, is one indication of expectations being met.

Everyone can hit a high score once in a while.

Consistently high scores on this question indicate an above average hospital.

Ninetieth percentile and above.

Watch this indicator.

Communication
Part One

56. Clear Channel

The most sought after ability among employers – communication – is also the most sought after among customers.

Master it, and your fortunes are assured in the State of Texas, or wherever you happen to reside.

If you are not a speechmaker, no worries.

You could be a master of body language, which could be considered the most important of the communication skills.

Or you may be very good at writing.

Or visual arts – graphic design.

Become a student of one of these.

Buy a lot of books on the subject – master it.

Then observe as you raise yourself to new heights.

Communicate.

57. Personal Approach

Your approach to the customer will determine if you approach success.

Whether it's your need for a higher satisfaction score, or a need to simply break the ice, approaching is the first step and always the key to customers.

This is your "first impression" – and reflects on you personally.

How do you improve the way a customer feels about YOU at first contact?

My tips:

"Dress For Success" by John Molloy – excellent book, and "New Women's Dress For Success" by same author.

Next – be humble.

Third – be a servant.

Fourth – keep your voice down and the conversation short.

Fifth – follow up and over-perform.

Being an expert on your service/product is also good.

Approach well or be toast.

58. It Starts With A Smile

You know how it is, when the check out clerk in Wal-Mart gives you a nice smile and "have a good day". This is probably the only interaction you will have at Wal-Mart.

May be the only smile somebody gave you the entire week.

The clerk just made you feel good, and worth the gold standard it is written on.

A ten second feel good from the cashier went straight to the heart.

The building costs millions to construct.

If it's a hospital, there are millions in equipment.

Perhaps there is $100 million riding on attracting customers.

But all the kings horses, along with his castle could not get the job done.

It was ten seconds from a clerk – that comes out to only pennies of labor time – to hook the customer.

Nobody knew save for the customer.

The customer came back the next Saturday, looking for that same clerk for another smile, but the employee was off and the customer found it in another. Another smiling clerk.

This is what people look for. To feel good, to feel comfortable.

Somebody that may even have some good news to tell.

Good relations start with smiles.

59. Working Hectic

In this store, store clerk Sally was at unease as the line grew long at her checkout register.

Fifteen people were now in line, and the wait was at least 10 minutes.

Sally had no smile.

Sally's frantic pace to get the line down showed on her face.

Sally's manager had said that sales were slightly down, and a co-worker was laid off.

She did not understand this, because an extra checkout clerk was actually needed.

After the co-worker was laid off, sales went down even further.

There was not much to smile about around here.

Hectic paces can bring frowning faces.

If you have this working atmosphere, you have to somehow bring on the smiles.

Bad thoughts and negativity will get the best of many people.

You cannot focus on anything except serving your customer.

For your customer, and for your survival.

60. Wasn't Issued To You For Laughs

Can you communicate with a child's toy and be effective?

Remember in the movie "The Longest Day", in which John Wayne gives a child's clicker toy to the soldiers.

The instructions were that, if a soldier could not identify another soldier whether American or German in the darkness of night, the toy could be clicked, as it made a loud "click" sound when pressed.

One click should be answered by two clicks. If not, the other person could be German.

This was based on actual events, and the child's toy perhaps saved lives on D-Day.

It was simple, but effective.

Simple but effective communication is exactly what customers want.

They want it simple, and with speed. A single image, the single quick sound of a click – can make or break the bank – and has the power to even save lives.

Be simple. Be quick. Be effective.

61. But Laughs Are Needed...

Humor is highly effective, and overlooked as one of the most dynamic communication abilities.

Everyone remembers a boss that was a humor-less manager.

They remember that for 8 hours every day, they watched the clock and all the men around them were dying to get out of that forsaken employer.

Give your workers plenty of humor.

They're bored out of their minds and need a gesture by you to get them through the day.

Find humor wherever it can be found.

Use it often.

Laughter inspires production.

STAFF DEVELOPMENT

62. Setting Priorities.

"Labor is prior to, and independent of, capital. Capital is only the fruit of labor, and could never have existed if labor had not first existed. Labor is the superior of capital, and deserves much the higher consideration".

– ABRAHAM LINCOLN

This quote is not about political beliefs, it's about priorities.

Lincoln explained the importance of labor in his Dec 3, 1861 State of the Union address.

The total focus of a business should be on its people?

The actual focus of a business should be whatever it takes to make the thing work.

What makes it work is people plus money – they go together.

Lincoln says here the owner of the business, and the people under the owner have to go to work before any money is produced.

How true.

In housekeeping, focusing on what that work is can help the business of the hospital make the capital needed.

Focus on helping the workers to be their best, to produce fruit.

63. Setting A Tone

A comedian was once asked what it was like to guest host the

Johnny Carson Show.

"Even if your dog just died", the comedian replied, "you have to go out there and make everyone smile".

This is something very difficult to do, but essential.

If you start the day off in a just-okay mood, everyone will follow your lead. You're the leader.

They will take your non-smile and transfer that to the customer. The customer gets a just-okay, average attitude from the service person.

Even if something is not going right in your life, you must set the tone. You can sometimes clock out early and take a break, if that's what it takes to re-set your own mood.

But setting the tone for the day starts early in the morning.

Every day, bring on the positive. Early.

64. Jumbo Jet Energy

"There are miracles in life I must achieve
But first I know it starts inside of me"

– R. KELLY

The people working around you that possess the most energy are also most likely your highest producers.

Trying to find out what everybody's psychology is, get inside their heads, and then figure out how to boost their energy in their work – is, well…. possible, but not probable.

Many businesses take the people on staff with the most energy, give them a promise of some kind of reward, and then proceed to burn those people out.

Careful to avoid burnout.

How you find, build up, and harness the energy of your people will decide how much production you see through the year and coming years.

Find, among your staff, those that have a jet engine of energy that won't quit.

Somebody with a General Electric GE90 high-bypass turbofan engine with 115,000 lbs. of thrust. Somebody that has that, just needs a mere spark to set them off on a project exuberating a furious "get this done now" attitude.

If they don't have quite this much energy – my belief is that your high energy may rub off on them. They need a spark.

Give them a boost, get the projects done - then give them a rest.

Take care of these people, or they may fly away with their jet engine to another employer.

When they are going at full speed, however, give them room to accelerate for a time.

When called for, throw Nitro into the engine – open 'er up at full throttle.

Understand energy.

65. Southwest Airlines – people first

Southwest Airlines success story should be studied by anyone serious about learning business.

Two E's –

Empowerment and Education are key reasons for their success, according to many business articles.

Turning loose the creative power that people yearn to let out and shine.

To be allowed to innovate.

Education is critical. Expensive, but a must.

Read about Southwest Airlines.

66. What happens when satisfaction scores go down.

Sometimes a boss will look for paperwork and figures – plus graphs and charts of any kind.

He needs a Powerpoint presentation to show what went wrong.

When all along, maybe offering a helping hand to the front line people could benefit.

It's the housekeeper, volunteer, dietary aide, CNA that drive many of the perceptions in the hospital. In a retail store, it's the cashier, floor clerk.

Because they are on the front lines, directly in front of the customer; in many cases, it's the least paid people that drive your customer satisfaction scores, and your business.

These workers are working to help your customer.

Step in and show them how proud you are of them.

They're waiting for a leader to come in and really show them a few rays of sunshine.

They're waiting for you.

Take care of them. Reach out to the least paid.

67. Be In Their Shoes

Somebody says – "Do we just need another Fish book, and that's all?"

(Fish! A Proven Way to Boost Morale and Improve Results by Stephen C. Lundin, John Christensen, and Ken Blanchard, March 8, 2000)

Well, first, you may have read the Fish book and moved on to other books.

The associates may have never heard of it.

So for them, if we can apply some of the principles in the Fish book – this may be ten times more attention than they are getting now.

The most damaging assumptions are the ones I don't even know

I'm making.

If I assume a book is outdated and not worth the look, I'd have to say that well, the Bible is kind of old, but not outdated, and still worth a look.

So there may be something there in older business books.

The workers may need these ideas you covet, but nobody is sharing with them.

Understanding the worker's needs, does take up some of your personal time.

You have to understand them to be in their shoes.

68. This Hospital Is Not A Pink House

Many people out there may have a music selection on an I-pod or a computer, the song by John Mellencamp, his "Pink Houses" song.

I'm one of them.

Although I've always liked the song, it's kind of depressing.

The lyrics give an impression of how life can pass you by with no meaning. Just living in a little house with perhaps and interstate highway within 50 feet of your front door, no major accomplishments, a life of austerity, and how somebody joked that someday you'd be President.

It would be funny if not so real for many people.

This is the life they may be living at work – unless you as a manager determine that this is not to be.

They *will not* come into this place of work thinking that it's a meaningless job, that it's kind of depressing, that there are no accomplishments to be had here; and there is some kind of joke about not really measuring up.

Bullcorn.

They are indeed accomplishing major pieces of work, and their work is recognized and taken seriously.

A dynamic manager will work on creating an atmosphere that each individual feels like they're part of something big, part of a team that cares, working for "the real thing", even if you're not Coca-Cola, and builds up the esteem of our hard working people out there.

Mellencamp's song is a good artistic work, but make sure your work place is not helping to fulfill the meaning of the lyrics. Instead, give them Willie Nelson's "Blue Skies".

Blue skies uplift.

69. Motivation Can't Be Managed

You need to motivate your workers, but it is not about "managing".

"Managing", means to keep under control something you have control over.

You can manage an inventory, but *"people don't want to be managed, they want to be led"*, said the author Zig Ziglar.

To motivate, change the atmosphere.

Create a place where workers can motivate themselves.

You could be the one that travels outside of the bubble called "life you are in", and create a different atmosphere for **yourself**, so they will view you as someone reaching out.

Reaching out for them.

I suggest to enter their world, and talk their language/ walk their shoes, with the following example:

Music is an international language.

Share music with your workers – it breaks barriers between you and them.

Use the internet.

If it's Spanish, check out Spanish/Tejano radio.

If it's Nepal, check out Nepali radio.

Even sleepy eyed, they may perk up when the volume goes up.

The atmosphere is created, and they feel like their boss understands their world.

Zig Ziglar said that employees want to work for a manager whose competence and concern they can trust.

The concern part – you really have to reach out to show you care.

They know their manager must be concerned, if he/she took the trouble to learn something dear to them.

The different cultures of music you may find refreshing also.

Cultivate yourself, motivate the staff.

70. It's About Respect

A horse is pretty sensitive.
A horse can feel a mosquito land on his butt in a
windstorm"

– BUCK BRANNAMAN

Professional horseman and consultant on the movie "Horse Whisperer"

Buck Brannaman can take an out of control horse, and make him calm down in a matter of minutes.

Many people witness this, and can't see how it's possible.

In the documentary "Buck", he describes that his approach to horses is one of feelings; it's a matter of respecting the horse, and the horse calms down.

Humans are pretty sensitive also.

They will respond to your approach, and they can feel a fly on their neck in a windstorm.

When you respect an animal or a human, the respect reciprocates.

71. Half Hearted

"Look, here comes somebody with some pizza", says one of the associate workers.

The associates do get some good food.

They are happy for an hour – this is good.

Then the grinding day starts again.

The company they work for is still a bungling, mistake prone, with half-hearted measures and blind alleys to nowhere kind of company.

The workers look for the lady in the Calgon bubble bath commercial to come and take them away.

Somebody remembers some pizza twice a year.

A few pizzas, a few decades of service.

This is not the dynamic place it could have been, and it's not something a committee full of people checking their cell phones can make better.

It takes more.

72. Harvey Mackay's Story

In his book, "Swim With The Sharks Without Being Eaten Alive", Harvey Mackay gives us a dose of what is required by each individual to really make a difference that can stand out.

He tells the story about one day hailing a cab, and the driver pulled up in a highly polished car, jumped out wearing a tie, and opened the door for Harvey.

Once inside, the driver asked Harvey if he would like to read a newspaper.

He had drinks, radio stations – everything Harvey needed for his ride.

Also – the cab was spotlessly clean inside.

Harvey was shocked by this level of service from a cab driver.

The man mentioned that his business was way up, and mostly his customers were by appointment only now.

What a story this is; how a person can take what many consider a low end, low paying job and start making a better living by improving the service and the environment of his customers.

A cab driver took service and environment improvement to the extreme, and had his story printed in one of the top business books of all time.

Service plus Environment = A winning combination.

73. Going The Distance

Phil Collins recently made a stop in Abilene, Texas to receive an honorary doctor of history degree from McMurry University.

He was being honored for his interest in Texas history, particularly the battle of the Alamo. Collins new book, "The Alamo and Beyond: A Collectors Journey", was aided by McMurry professors Don Frazier and Steve Hardin.

Collins is one of three artists, along with Paul McCartney and Michael Jackson, to have sold more than 100 million albums as both a solo artist and member of a band.

What is it that would bring this level of artist to a small town, to write a book?

"The courage of those at the Alamo and the struggle for liberty ring true for me", Collins said.

Collins has been fascinated with the story since boyhood, with TV's Davy Crockett and John Wayne's "The Alamo".

Perhaps also, it is the story about people willing to go the distance, do "whatever it takes" for the task at hand, as the defenders of The Alamo faced certain death for liberty and freedom.

"Whatever it takes" is powerful enough to interest and lure many people, and is a true motivator.

Tell your people – "whatever it takes".

74. Myers Briggs

The Myers Briggs personality test (myersbriggs. org) can be helpful to those looking for insight into different personalities and behaviors.

It's an exercise in better understanding how other people think.

This knowledge can keep conflicts down, and places you in a better awareness, aiding in your quest to continually uplift the people around you.

Understand better.

75. Find Some Luck

Pot-luck lunches are way under-rated.

Many times, they help build team spirit, and that's something you cannot get enough of.

Hold these as often as time allows.

Luck is in a pot.

76. Blank Walls/Blank Stares

"They came in, with faces of defeat that serious men would give applause. Sad faces are always good, they reasoned; gray skies with purple outlines faded out disappearing sunshine, and the serious men knew despair would echo off these plain white walls of yesteryear".

Does your place of business read like a novel filled with desperate characters of no hope?

Are there cork bulletin boards in the break room, thumb tacks holding drooped over papers that nobody reads; and the papers date from three years ago?

Are the walls blank, with nothing but the plain white enamel which shows its decades old texture, resembling perhaps an abandoned building from 30 years ago?

Maybe there is one picture hanging – a cheap copy of a cheap painting by a failed artist that lived in the 1890's - a scene of faded out green colors, the usual tree & shrub, looks like it should have been burned in the college bonfire; and it's been hanging in the same spot for the last 8 years.

Also, sitting on a dusty side table, a trophy where somebody won a softball game 15 years ago. The furniture, looking like it was pulled out from under a highway bridge, actually was pulled out of a run down warehouse, this furniture resurrected to see another decade of doldrums before the next manager that's had enough decides to take it back to the warehouse.

When someone has a seat in this business, a psychological effect on the human brain takes its toll as an inner voice starts to subconsciously whisper to this seated person; "I need to get away for a while – things are bugging me around here and I'm not sure what it is."

My advice here is to think about sprucing up your break room/office/business a bit, before these events can occur.

Lose the bummed out boring atmosphere. Motivate the staff.

77. Home Could Be Here

Some of your associates may be in a dreary situation outside of work.

They may count on the positives found at work to get through the day, and for them this work place may be kind of a second home.

Direct them to a fulfilling work day.

They count on you. Encouragement may turn them into the highest performers – all because of you, because you could see the situation and knew what they needed.

Encourage.

78. Where's My Girl

"We are ladies and gentlemen serving ladies and gentlemen".

– Ritz-Carlton Hotel Company motto

People should be called by their name, or a respectful reference.

The word "girl" is a flattering term when used by friends talking about friends.

I've seen it used by people from the UK in a business atmosphere.

In an American business setting, "lady", or simply the name of the female is best choice.

Through my years in hospitals, I've occasionally had someone ask "where's my cleaning girl?"

I've had them use this about a lady that was 50 years old.

This is not respectful, even if the female is of young years of age.

Lose the word "girl" in referring to anyone professionally in a hospitality business, and leave "girls" and "boys" on the playground.

We are ladies and gentlemen.

This is a business of respect.

YOURSELF

79. Drivin' Your Attitude

What is it that pushes top performers to keep driving without hitting the brakes?

Maybe nobody really knows, but I know the attitude has to come from inside them.

I think it's kind of "not losing hope", and believing that all odds will not defeat you, even if you are not number one.

It's just the never stopping, never quitting till death.

Eventually, something has to give in. There will be success.

It may take 30 years to show something.

Patience and discipline.

Get back on track and you can't stop, if you want to be undefeated in spirit.

Ask for God's help.

Don't stop.

80. Daring, But Not Reckless

"Gentlemen, this school is about combat. There are no points for second place."

– TOP GUN, THE MOVIE

Following procedures has its place, and is totally necessary when it comes to safety.

But, creativity is also totally necessary to excel above the crowd.

If you are a creative person, use it and be different when it comes to things like new approaches to a customer, handling employee situations, promoting your cause.

Taking chances, safely, can give you a trial and error method that can produce amazing results.

You must try new things to find improvement areas.

Many old methods are still solid, and the best way.

Seek the Top, seek a pioneer spirit.

81. The Already Been There/Done That Method

Many people look out over satisfaction scores, and wonder how to peak above average.

Old methods of reaching the customer, have been successful, so it would seem best to do that.

In most cases, it probably is.

The matter here is that, everyone has already heard of that way of doing things, and those ways have been hammered to the customer for about a decade now.

You may not be able to rise above the crowd by practicing the exact same thing that all the other folks in the United States have known about and drilled down for 10 or 20 years.

You would be merely doing the same thing that everyone else is doing, so you may come up with the average scores that everyone else produces.

Now, you can take an old method and just be a superstar – take that thing and go all the way.

Or, you can take a small trial and try this new idea you've been itching to talk to your customer/patient about – see if they like this new way to make them comfortable.

The things that have to be approved by a supervisor, well that's okay.

You are really wanting to help the guest, so don't give up. Get your idea approved if needed, and make your customer very happy.

Enthusiasm is good.

82. Risk Taking:

"It's the order you disobey that makes you famous"

– GENERAL DOUGLAS MACARTHUR

When Colonel MacArthur was told by a General to advance on the Germans in

World War I, MacArthur requested to lead his men into battle. This was unusual, as the custom was to stay behind lines for a high ranking officer.

MacArthur was granted his request. But then, he did not wear the usual Army uniform; instead of a helmet, wore his soft hat. Wore riding breeches instead of Army issue pant.

A soldier questioned this, and MacArthur gave his famous quote.

After the battle, a journalist published that "Colonel MacArthur is one of the ablest officers in the United States Army and also one of the most popular."

Should you disobey orders?

Well, not when it comes to healthcare policy – we all have to uphold those.

I think the idea here is to think like a pioneer when problems need resolving.

Seems like something always comes up where we have to think on our feet, something that is not specifically a policy.

For example, how to be the best representative for this hospital that you can be.

There are books written on customer service.

How to be more knowledgeable in your job.

There are books written on your line of work.

Books also on how to learn a different language. There are books on that.

Or you may just want to come in, when you are called to battle, with a new attitude of "let's get it done – I'm leading the charge", like MacArthur.

Wearing a different hat on that day was MacArthur's attitude maker.

Seemed to help him for that one occasion. Must have gave him something psychologically he needed to get the job done.

To get that pioneer spirit, you must be confident that yes, you can explore new ideas within a safety realm.

When it comes to customer comfort, I don't think anyone will object if you try to improve that.

There are proven methods, but only one unique approach that comes from your personality when you are in front of the customer.

Look for ways to improve.

INFECTION CONTROL

83. A nosocomial infection is known as a hospital acquired infection.

In other words, a patient ends up being attacked by germs that already existed *inside* the hospital.

The Centers for Disease Control estimates that about 1.7 million hospital associated infections contribute to 99,000 deaths each year in the US.

Surface sanitation is one of the components used to break the cycle of nosocomial disease.

There is tons of information out there on this subject.

It's good to close down a room and give it a good scrub down even if someone has to wait an additional twenty minutes.

"Tried and true" methods should be upheld, but there is also an element that says we have to think on our feet to reduce the infections.

A policy to disinfect a surface is a must, but going beyond that is necessary many times.

If you can't see the enemy, overkill on cleaning is just a better approach.

A good manager standing in the forefront of this battle, should take the initiative, place themselves on the line and say "stop."

"Stop, because we have to clean this area, room, floor, wall, chair, anything – better than the standard cleaning in this case."

Take courage, ask for a "stop" when needed.

84. May the force be with you, but at least the guys in that movie could see the enemy.

The hospital team with direct patient care; nurses, doctors – are fighting germs which are an unseen, invisible enemy.

The housekeeper's fight this same enemy on surfaces.

Finding an invisible man would be child's play compared to finding an eliminating all germs.

The invisible man is only one man.

You don't even know when you've killed the bacteria which is why we work to disinfect all high touch surfaces just to be sure.

Housekeeping fights a far more sinister villain than any super villain in an Iron Man comic book.

Housekeepers do a pretty good job attacking these pathogens.

Housekeepers are defenders, and the cleaners and disinfectants they use, are on the front lines of defense.

"Good offense wins games, and good defense wins championships"

Vince Lombardi

In the fight against bacteria on surfaces, good defense has even more meaning than it does in a Super Bowl game; it means that people get to stay healthy.

The "Force" is not with us. We need to come off our coffee break and attack, with brushes, cleaners, and elbow grease on every surface we can lay a hand on.

We are each an Army of One against the unseen.

85. Scrub With Bubbles Plus A Brush

Some cleaning methods may become outdated as time goes along.

One in particular is the attempt to use a single disinfectant to clean all surfaces in a hospital, with no other products allowed.

Hospital disinfectants are typically mixed at 256:1 with water.

This is one part chemical with 256 parts water – or one ounce chemical in two gallons of water.

This mixture is almost all water, and while the disinfectant can kill the germs listed on the label, under laboratory settings, something else is needed in actual use.

The mixture has almost no cleaning ability; slightly heavier cleaners may be needed on some surfaces to use first and remove surface soils.

Even the instructions that go with the disinfectant recommends to clean heavy surface soils before use of the disinfectant.

Remove all soils first – the absence of soil is more desirable than a false sense the surface is free of germs because a chemical was applied.

Scrutinize methods.

86. New Tech On Germs

The new luminesce sprays and ATP (adenosine triphosphate) swabs are an excellent way to "see" germs on a surface. These may become more affordable over time.

They are an awesome way to collect data, share with your staff, educate all of us in this battle on the unseen.

COMMUNICATION
PART TWO:

YOUR MESSAGE TO THE CUSTOMER

87. Communicate With Passion

Ever stayed in a hotel where they left chocolate on
the pillow?

What did this communicate?

It said that the hotel cared enough to spend
time on even the most finite detail to ensure your
happiness.

While chocolate in a hospital cannot be done since some patients are not allowed food before surgery, or sweets of any kind – other forms of showing off your master of detail can be displayed.

Ever thought of leaving a business card with a note for the incoming patient?

Maybe you could simply write "I'm here for you, I'm your housekeeping representative", and "here is my number".

As you do this, there will be responses. You may not see them, but the difference you make to the patient by doing this cannot be measured so easily or expressed in words.

There will be returns for your hard work – the patient had someone that cared for them, helping them when they needed it.

The reward will be knowing you did this.

88. Shock em'

"People won't stand in line to watch me pull rabbits out of a hat"

– SOUND BITE FROM MOVIE "HOUDINI".

Magicians know they have to go big. They have to think big, and they have to surprise the customer.

Making a jet airplane disappear was done years ago by David Copperfield.

Well, we don't do magic, but the lesson is that in order to win satisfaction, we have to understand that the expectations are very high from the American people.

They're used to seeing, hearing, tasting - amazing things.

The one thing that can continue to satisfy even the most hardened people – is that of a personal touch.

A personal note, a personal visit, a personal word of encouragement.

The words in marketing are surprise and shock.

We are surprised and shocked so much, we are beyond responding to most of it anymore.

You know what the biggest surprise may be?

Arranging an atmosphere where the customer/patient is left alone *and* comfortable.

You now see Sandals.com running multitudes of ads, showing people sitting on beaches and for the most part removed *from* hectic workplaces, enjoying personal comfort.

Espouse electricity – shock em'.

Do it by arranging an "I'll give you silence for a while" environment.

BUT, they are not left alone in a room of boredom.

A note, something to read, and a personal visit.

The personal touch still shocks people.

89. A Story To Remember

Overheard: Lady says to another lady, "did you see that commercial with the squirrels? It's so funny – I don't remember which company it was, but it sure was funny".

This potential customer was made to feel good, but she could not recall what was being sold.

The lady was entertained, but the ad was useless to convince.

The same lady could probably tell you in which building Cary Grant was supposed to meet --- in the famous movie "An Affair To Remember".

The movie was made in 1957, but the story was remembered.

The lady remembered what happened to Cary at the top of the Empire State Building.

People remember stories, but they mostly forget names of companies that just "put out a message" of quality service.

The message with a compelling story about YOU, not clowning squirrels, may be better.

90. Sale Made In Three Seconds

Time is short.

People check their phones, watches.

You may not have time to show a Harrison Ford movie to convince.

Everyone is bombarded with ads to attract their attention.

Movie trailers use images less than one second long to convince public the movie is worth watching.

Convincing – with super- fast images – is the new medium.

The images must be so edited down to the core, that a few images can tell the story, and be believable.

A single photograph, a single graphic, may be able to tell your story.

What photo can you take that will do that.

Which graphic, or two or three graphics, will convince in three seconds.

An image is quick, and may tell a story.

91. Process of Irritation Elimination

If you are not sure how to begin a process to improve your environment, first start by eliminating the irritations.

Walk through each room, area, floor, and look for things that are potentially irritating – then remove them.

Blemishes on the walls, unsightly, peeling paint, old brackets that used to hold unknown objects, poor lighting – countless other things – remove them.

Eliminate irritations.

92. The Ritz

"A person's name is to that person the sweetest and most important sound in any language", according to the author Dale Carnegie.

It's funny how some of the most successful businesses have taken that to heart.

Ritz Carlton, a hotel famous for making people comfortable, lists what they train their employees as "Three Steps Of Service".

The number one step is simply this:

"A warm and sincere greeting. Use the guest name, if and when possible."

Pretty simple.

Remember the TV show "Cheers?"

The song said "you want to go where everybody knows your name".

People tend to regard a place as highly treasured, when their name is known the moment they open the door.

Difficult to do because you have too many customers?

Perhaps.

But perhaps we can remember what kind of prices the Ritz is able to charge for those rooms, and come to the conclusion that the TV show Cheers was really correct.

Cheers ran for 11 years – very lengthy for a TV show.

Maybe people want to be part of a place like that.

Use the guest name, if and when possible.

93. Seismic Senses

Sight, Hearing, Touch, Smell, Taste.

The senses are powerful to each human.

Each customer is affected differently by each of the senses.

Out of these five areas, sight is probably the most powerful, with smell a close contender.

But that is hard to say, because to each his own.

Each hospital/company needs to think about a way to touch all senses.

Appealing to the senses, is indeed a comfort to your customer.

94. From these five

Out of the five, the irritations can be found.

So in addition to finding things that are unsightly, things that smell bad, things that are noisy, things that are unpleasant to touch, things that taste bad – find areas to improve these things in the customer experience.

If you are a hospital housekeeping manager, taste may not be something you can control.

That has to come from Dietary.

However, the other four are within your realm of persuasion.

Since sight is the strongest, eliminating eyesore's in your facility/rooms should be first.

Approach each room/area, look around and ask:
What are the obvious eyesore's here.
It's amazing what you will find.

Unsightly must be eliminated. Start with the obvious.

CUTS LIKE A KNIFE

95. Straight Through

This section cuts through all the nonsense and lists items for thought in a high performance building.

96. Quality Checks/Follow Up

The quality checks are the absolute pivotal point which will drive your quality standards. You set the standards, so you must be the one at the spearhead of quality checks.

Chef Ramsay (Hells Kitchen, Masterchef) does not stand back and allow a subordinate to perform all the checks for him. He is personally involved, up to his elbows.

If you need to design a checklist, so be it.

It's what you do about the findings, that determine the outcome.

Push quality checks to the max.

97. Furnishings – Sight Check # 1.

Broken chairs. Stained up chairs.

Over bed tables from the 1980's.

Bedside tables that look like they came out of a trash dump in South America.

Unfortunately, these can be found in some spots.

There must be a total commitment to upgrade, replace, fix, clean these furnishings to make your rooms/facility more presentable.

If your facility is out of cash, they may end up really and truly out of cash if they continue to hand a run down motel look to the customer.

Do what it takes.

98. Paint – Sight Check # 2.

A French interior decorator may not be available.

For a modest budget, not needed.

Painting covers over a multitude of sin. Fresh paint is relatively inexpensive compared to gutting an entire room.

Freshly caulked showers and sinks make an old restroom appear as if the management is taking care of things.

Fresh paint and caulk win over customers.

99. Cleanliness – Sight Check # 3.

Think of the cleanliness in your facility as your wardrobe.

When customers see your facility, they see your shirt/tie/dress/shoes.

If your customer walks through your hospital/business, and the floors have coffee/food stains, and the curtains are stained, and the restrooms are dirty; it's the same as a business owner spilling coffee/food all over themselves, then approaching the customer as if nothing has happened, with the owner appearing as if they just climbed out of a trash can and did not bother to shower and change clothes.

When an owner reaches out to shake hands, they cannot afford this kind of look.

When they see your facility, they see you.

100. Judgment That Hath No End

Mistakes are well hidden.

Incompetence is not easily discerned by customers.

Except when it comes to cleanliness.

The work of a housekeeper cannot be hidden – everything is in plain sight.

A guest may not be able to realize many things, but they can see, 24 hours a day, if the room is clean.

A patient lying in a bed for a day or a week, will laser beam focus on every speck of work of the housekeeper – there is no hiding it.

One spot on the ceiling will cancel the deal – this place is dirty!

A single hair in a corner can draw the attention of a visiting guest.

People know cleanliness more than any other task the hospital can perform.

Patients willing to recommend your hospital/ business, more often than naught, may rest on these observations.

After non-stop, 24/7 judgment on cleanliness, the patient will decide if they want to return to your facility.

Clean.

101. Wet Floor Signs

Yellow wet floor signs may be your judgment.

The same is said about a business card.

When they see your business card, it may be the only piece of info they have to make a judgment about whether to do business or not.

In housekeeping, our yellow "wet floor" signs are our business card.

They are bright yellow for safety, and they are noticed because of that color.

Everyone knows they belong to the housekeeping department.

A housekeeper placed them there.

When people see these yellow signs, they see housekeeping.

If a sign is dirty, this sends a signal that the entire facility may be dirty, and to be avoided.

That's why I insist that all Wet Floor signs are kept spotlessly clean.

Wet floor signs are the business card for housekeeping.

102. Building Fragrance - Check # 1.

You are judged on smells and fragrances.

If your hospital/business smells with a foul odor, you may as well call the cows home – it's over.

Nursing homes are notorious for unpleasant smells. Engage your average American on the subject of nursing homes, and very soon a comment will come up about smells.

God bless the residents and workers of nursing homes. They deserve an exceptional home.

It's not that they can't control odors – it just takes a lot of work and yes, money – to make that happen.

When people are alerted to a foul odor in any business – they judge the business on it.

Fragrances are exceptionally, and highly overlooked as a component that shapes the overall perceptions of hospitals, buildings, businesses, and their owners.

Never underestimate fragrance.

103. Public Restroom Fragrance - Check # 2

Your most powerful fragrances should be installed, sprayed, used continuously in public restrooms, but not overused. Finding a good balance can be difficult.

Simply spraying a can of deodorant is only a temporary fix in high use restrooms.

Deodorizing a public restroom properly can be misunderstood as an easy task that can be solved by automatic dispensers.

Public restrooms, especially in older buildings, are difficult to keep clean and keep fragranced properly.

This is a golden opportunity. Providing the best possible fragrances in public restrooms can truly shock and awe your customer.

People are begging us to have a good smelling restroom.

Bouquet your restrooms.

104. Patient Rooms – Fragrance Check # 3

Would it kill anybody to occasionally offer a fragrance to a patient?

And the tremendous cost of giving out a can of premium deodorant?

Three dollars.

105. Chef Ramsay and a Good Burger.

Gordon Ramsay has been asked the secret to winning Michelin stars in his famed restaurants.

The one word he used to sum up this achievement – consistency.

No matter what time of the day, the food remains very high quality.

Consistency works as a catalyst in any business, even burgers & fries.

Whataburger, with about 700 locations in the southern half of US, serves up a consistent excellent burger 24 hours a day. The fries are always fresh, no matter what time you walk in.

Not an easy task, since Whataburger restaurants are never closed.

Most locations also bring the burger with a tray of condiments & napkins right out to your table, as if to say "We will offer high quality & service, 24 hours, consistently".

Many business can get the first two items down; they can offer quality, they can be open extended hours, but to offer quality all the time?

Consistency raises the bar into outer space.

Reach your highest quality, and be consistent.

Bidders & Figuring

106. Landscaping Scenario

A request bid for landscaping services in Denver is faxed to a contractor in Kansas City.

Fifty acres of land are to be serviced.

The contractor uses a simple method on price per square footage.

He dreams of using his large tractor mower to quickly knock out the grass, and his bid is based on using that tractor to achieve cheapest price. He is also very experienced and knows the average price per square foot that most contractors charge.

After winning the bid, he panics when he discovers the fifty acres are covered with tree stumps and rocks, plus a stream of water flows through the middle.

He will be unable to use his large machine to quickly knock out the job – this will take twice as much labor as anticipated.

Additionally, the owner of the land has allowed a group of scientists to study wildlife on the property, and they cannot be disturbed on the days they are there.

Since the contractor must meet the obligation, he must schedule landscaping to be performed at midnight on those days, driving up his labor costs and requiring him to purchase additional equipment.

The requirement is to stay within the budget, so he decides to just lower the quality of his work to keep the business, say nothing to the customer and hopes nobody will notice.

Similarly, basing custodial bids on square footage alone is a flaw in the way some bids are done.

Many factors must be considered, and each hospital/business is unique to the land.

Square footage bidding using general numbers considers only part of the necessary information.

107. I'll Bid For Your Dinner.

Your family decides a nice restaurant outing is in order.

Specifications are faxed to bidders.

The winning bid is 3 cents per plate less than next to lowest.

The low bid comes from a gas station, and offers a plate of food but with no table or chairs.

You end up eating on the floor at an all night gas station.

Could this really happen? Would you go with the cheapest bid on food and eat on the floor to save money?

Similar circumstance;

A business decides a housekeeping contractor would be nice.

Specifications are sent out.

Winning bid is 3 cents per square foot less than next to lowest.

You end up with gas station cleanliness & ambience.

Cheaper bids are good for cost containment, but specs may not be upheld, and you don't realize what happened till it's really too bad.

A dinner table is right in front of your eyes – something directly in your presence is easier to judge.

A million sq ft hospital? Mostly out of sight most of the time to building owners.

When the neglect is finally realized, it will take years to catch up.

Make thorough checks on whom you hire to contract.

How Many People to Clean

108. Just Tell Me What It Costs

In the example of building a home, many measurements and factors have to be plugged in to get the best estimate on finished cost.

All the costs of labor and materials need factoring in.

The same way in cleaning a building; if an estimator merely walks through a million square foot hospital and can come up with a custodial bid in a few hours, the chance is great the bid will be off.

It will be a bid, and the company can start cleaning.

But, if simple generalities on the math numbers were applied, and the bidders made little attempt to communicate details to the customer, there could be trouble soon.

It takes detail planning and communication

109. Rose Colored Glasses Meets An Accountant

This section is not about an accountant that tries to see how cheap a bid can be done.

Given that the cheapest bid can end up in complete an utter failure to produce a clean hospital, this section is about looking at what the true cost can be (in FTE's, *full time employees*) to get to a state of *crystal clean* patient rooms.

A building owner may take a shrewd, honest look at where they are in the process and where they want to be.

A manager must do the same, and work within the budget given.

The questions to ask are these:

– What level of customer satisfaction are we seeking, and to what level or depth are we willing to pursue to achieve the number one slot in customer satisfaction.

– Are we really dedicating enough resources for our housekeeping department to do the job, or are we looking through rose tinted glasses, throwing just enough, but not enough.

– Finally, if we use a calculator with real numbers, are we willing to accept the findings.

The way to get real numbers in this business is to ask questions, lots of them.

And then observe!

If you have personally worked in housekeeping, many questions are already answered.

In any case, a questionnaire is in order to get the information you need.

Let the analysis begin.

110. Square Footage vs Adjusted Patient Days

Many hospitals use the square footage method.

This method is excellent, but can fail depending on the details.

Using the scenario of a home buyer looking to build a home:

The buyer asks a home builder what price a new fifteen hundred square foot home would cost.

The builder, using the square footage method, pulls out a calculator and quickly tells you a new home with that square footage will cost $100 per square foot. If he has asked no further questions about any details you would like in your new home, the method will produce less accuracy than desired.

However, if all details are laid in, this can be the excellent method.

Some hospitals use the Adjusted Patient Day method.

With this method, and using the scenario of a home builder again as an example - the builder asks you how many people will be living in your home. With that, he uses a calculator and tells you that with 4 people living in your home, the cost to build your home will be X number of dollars per person, depending on how much time these people will spend in the home.

As you can see, the adjusted patient days method may not hold well up under real numbers.

It measures how many patients are in the hospital, then provides an answer based on that.

It does not take into account the square footage, and that all areas still must be cleaned except for the variance in patient rooms, because all areas still have trash cans that must be pulled, floors that must be swept, mopped, and restrooms cleaned.

It does not take into account all the other operations going on 24 hours a day which call for housekeeping services.

It also does not take into account all non-patient areas being cleaned which are not affected by a patient variance.

It does not take into account discharge cleaning, which may actually increase with lesser patient counts, because nursing will transfer many patients around in the empty rooms that are available to get them situated in just the right room, usually closer to the nurses station. Just a little increase in transfers and discharges may eclipse any perceived savings of labor hours due to a smaller census. Those extra transfer rooms must be cleaned, no matter the census.

It also does not take into account the size of the hospital.

Some hospitals have more office space than others, and some hospitals have a large campus with buildings spread over 50 or 100 acres.

Environmental Services encompasses the entire building and campus, not just patient rooms.

Whichever method is used, great detail is needed for success.

7 Components

111. The Square Foot Route

The following pages contain information if you decide the square foot method is right for you.

112. 7 Components

There are seven components I have used to help understand how many full time employees I need to clean a large hospital, and to what level.

They are:
1. Unitizing
2. Measuring

3. Production Rate Research
4. Verify Through Observation
5. Identify A Level Starting Point
6. Build A Spreadsheet
7. Take Action

Let's go through each part.

113. UNITIZING: Standard & Non - Standard

A Unit is how much space you are cleaning.

Units could be broken down into the very small, such as a single wash basin, to the very large, such as an entire building.

A wash basin, a toilet, a wall, a chair, or a room, are all measures of space.

There is no standard that requires hospitals to follow the same types of unit breakdowns as other hospitals.

Because of this, managers find it difficult to compare efficiencies from one hospital to another. If everyone is being measured by something different, it may be hard to say whom is doing well.

If you go into a hamburger restaurant, and the combo meal for a burger, fries, and drink cost $6.25, this is easy to measure against a competing burger restaurant, because combo meals are standard. It's usually a burger, fries, and drink. You already know how to measure that.

You can get a quote from several car repair shops in town on the cost of replacing a radiator on your car, because there is a measure standard already worked out on computer spreadsheets that allow the manager to figure a quick estimate.

If a custodial services bidder bids on cleaning an office building, he can count the standard items like how many offices and restrooms, and come up with a measure standard that is easy to bid with.

Most areas are cleaned once per night, and no more.

But when it comes to a hospital, much of the building and cleaning is not standard at all. There are unit spaces, but many areas need cleaning more than once per day, and in fact some need cleaning several times per day.

When you start throwing in Cath Lab's, Surgery, ER, blood and body fluids, isolation precautions – the standard is difficult because you can't standardize so easily the volume of body fluids that will need to be cleaned up, how much time you really may need for terminal cleans because the AORN (Association of periOperative Registered Nurses) standards are high, how much time you should allow for safety in handling regulated medical waste, how much time you will really need to spend on training.

You can't standardize how many drinks will be spilled, broken flower vases at the front door, extra warmer blankets needed in ER, pest control; this is not office building standards.

Also, there is no standard on when patients are healed up enough to leave the hospital – only God and the doctor can determine that.

These unpredictable movements of people called "checkouts", when a patient leaves the hospital, can sway your FTE requirements from zero to 60 in 5 seconds.

Patient discharges are a unit space standard that can sit still, or take off like a Ferrari, leaving your crew in the dust holding a hundred hours of work while much of the rest of the hospital clocks out, relieved their work is over for the night.

Here is something that is even more difficult to standardize:

Taking extra time to care for the patients that are sick.

Although a nursing function, housekeeping responds to extra needs also, and call lights can be answered by anyone.

Unitize a hospital with great care.

114. Small Units Or Large?

A Unit of space is as simple as a wash basin, a toilet, a floor.

Using a whole building as a unit is too large of a unit, and by the same token, using each single wash basin is too small of a unit.

Unitizing each wash basin and each tile on the wall is not reasonable.

So, giant units as well as miniature units are too extreme.

Conclusion:

Small to medium units will produce good results.

A public restroom is a good example of a medium unit.

Identify reasonable units

115. MEASURING: Units & Square Foot per Hour

Measuring:

If your room is 23' x 12', simply multiply the two measurements, and the square foot is 276'.

Square foot per hour:

Square foot (divided by) minutes required (times) 60 = square foot per hour.

A 276 sq ft room cleaned in a 20 minute time span:

276 (divided by) 20 minutes = 13.8 X 60 = **828 square foot per hour.**

116. Production Rates

After you have your units thought out, you need to know how long it takes to clean the new unit you just placed on Line 3 of an Excel Spreadsheet.

For example, the main atrium entrance of your hospital measures 60 feet by 50 feet, so how long should it take to mop this public entryway?

What you're looking for is a production rate.

How much time to clean a unit; per square foot.

I will give an idea on some production rates in the next few sections.

The answer to the production rate question is the most difficult item to find.

Contractors that spent a decade cleaning office buildings, may try to use the same thinking that was so successful to them in the past, and apply that to a large hospital.

The variables in hospitals are much greater than in offices.

It takes some time.

117. Production Rate Research

How much time is required to clean this room, floor, wall?

You need information, and lots of it.

This is the homework section.

You can go to www.issa.com. They have the "540 Cleaning Times", which can be of help.

There is one group of people with immense knowledge – your own custodians/housekeepers.

Get help from your own in-house custodian/housekeeper experts – they are the authority with experience to provide accurate information.

Info from other sources and well wishers may not be reliable, because as mentioned before – there are no hard and fast standards that can work accurately with every hospital, since all hospitals are different.

The accuracy must be spot on. A few degrees difference can steer an ocean liner hundreds of miles off course.

The combo meal - style quick reference is not there for hospital housekeeping.

Without a one-size-fits-all standard, the best authority on the subject is you and your team, working out a measurement system on your computer, in your facility.

Question authority.

118. What To Ask

Your own custodians/housekeepers are glad to answer questions.

If you have no housekeeping experience, no worries – all the info is there, waiting to be extracted from this wise group.

I suggest to hand out a questionnaire to all housekeepers and supervisors.

Sample questions:

1. How much time does it take to clean a restroom?
2. How much time to clean a restroom, and get it really clean?
3. How much time to clean a patient room – daily cleaning?
4. How much time to clean a patient daily clean, and get it really clean?
5. How much time to clean a patient room – discharge checkout cleaning?
6. How much time to clean a nurses break room?
7. Do you sweep/mop all your hallways, or just spot mop?
8. How much time to spot sweep/mop all your hallways?

If the answer on daily room cleaning is 10 minutes by one housekeeper, and another housekeeper's answer is 15 minutes, your average is 12.5 minutes.

119. Verify Through Observation

The answers you get on these questions will vary of course.

If you have a supervisor, collaborate with them on narrowing the times down to an average. Then check.

Take time to observe your housekeeper times. Are they a close match?

Watch and time housekeepers cleaning the areas.

Then, your most crucial observation comes in.

Are the restrooms, patient rooms, nurses break rooms, really *that* clean?

Are the walls clean?

Are your floors clean?

Are the corners clean?

Would it pass in a 4 or 5 star hotel?

Observe.

120. Identify A Level Starting Point

Now, record the average of the times you are working at now.

Then assign yourself a Level that reflects your cleaning times & performance.

If we give that Levels 1 through 4 are the four levels, with Level 1 being the lowest, what Level would you give yourself?

If it's a Level 2, then you may make a statement that, while you are not at the bottom on Level 1, you have much work to do if you want to achieve Level 3, or the impossible Level 4.

To get to Level 3, you will need to again ask questions, observe, then add the amount of time needed to achieve your goal – the times you figured were necessary to achieve the next step in quality.

I assume you will need to add more time to achieve a higher goal.

But, you may identify an area where time is not used wisely, and can be taken away and placed in another area to help your averages.

If Level 2 is where you are now, Level 3 is where you want to go.

Your level of cleanliness is your current standard.

121. Why Different Levels?

– *"Step by step. I can't see any other way of accomplishing anything".*

From the book "I can't Accept Not Trying" by Michael Jordan

In his book, *I Can't Accept Not Trying*, Jordan talks about improving your game one step at a time.

He said that, he could not become the top player in the league immediately.

First, he had to recognize the level he was at, then improve upon that level one step at a time, through hard work and practicing relentlessly.

Similarly, we cannot become the most clean hospital in the district immediately.

We have to recognize the level we are at, then improve upon that level one step at a time.

In Jordan's case, the playing field is understood in that 5 players are against

5 players. The FTE's needed to play the game of basketball is figured out.

Each basketball court is exactly the same size, and the rules are that 10 guys will play on the exact same sized court with the exact same rules every time.

In hospital housekeeping, such an easy matchup of the rules is not so obvious.

Every hospital is a different size, with different requirements.

So there are two ways to improve: working on our personal achievements, but to also understand the labor requirements of our hospital's unique sized square footage and unique areas.

Using square footage, backed by different cleaning times depending on the area, plus cleanliness inspections, we can begin to see a more clear picture on what level we are playing, and with that, determine FTE requirements.

Game On.

122. I Have A Clean Hospital And Few FTE's

You may have very few people working in the housekeeping department, and at the same time have a very clean hospital.

If you are in this situation, you are to be congratulated.

Unfortunately, not many hospitals enjoy an accomplishment like that.

Trying to find a balance that can achieve the goal without expending an overt amount of labor time is the holy grail in treasure seeker lore.

You may have an outstanding crew that clean faster and better than Michael Phelps can swim, but it's not likely.

Michael Phelps was at top physical peak when winning those gold medals.

Then, after a period of time, Phelps cannot win those medals anymore – he is past his time.

Crews that are not in their physical peak anymore, including this author, have to be motivated – and everyone in housekeeping is working in a department in which a good percentage of the priority is physical work.

This is not to discount experience or customer service skills.

To the contrary – those skills are essential.

But the physical part of the work, is the very essence of housekeeping.

The charts I placed in the next few pages are a guide for those seeking some kind of place to start in the never ending FTE questions.

123. Level Descriptions

I found it very helpful to name my Level, to give it a name besides Level 1,2,3,4.

Identify it, call it for what it is.

The travel web sites use the numbers from 1 through 5 for customer reviews for a hotel, with 5 being the highest score.

To challenge myself, a number was not good enough.

I wanted a description for the low score I would give myself, to be a name that would knock the wind out of me, and motivate me that I would never be at that level.

On the flip side, I wanted the highest level name to reward myself, if I dare approached that lofty goal.

So these are the levels:

Marriott Hotel -   Level 4
Motel 6 -   Level 3
Gas Station -   Level 2
Horse Stable -   Level 1

I call these "word pictures", because with these short descriptions, you can easily bring to mind what kind of cleanliness could be found at these particular kinds of locations.

Who wants to be cleaning at the level of a gas station?

Motel 6 should be the minimum goal.

Motel 6 is a nice hotel chain, and provides at least a decent room, decent cleanliness for the price.

Marriott hotel type of cleanliness is the ultimate goal, but can it be reached consistently?

Naming levels with a word picture, can challenge those that like to be challenged.

124. Build A Chart (In Excel)

If you do not have access to a work loading software application from a good source, then join the club. But you can build and customize your own.

Building your own has the advantage of really getting personally involved in the numbers, and understanding them as you go along.

The following charts are just a guide. You will see that, in Level 1, this person spent almost no time on the corridors, and 11 minutes on a waiting room/ restroom.

Nonetheless, the area added up to 6.43 hours.

Since Level 1 is the lowest cleaning level, giving this person more time to clean ends up going beyond an 8 hour shift.

The first four charts are from a nursing unit, showing all the levels.

Disclaimer:

Adjust cleaning times as fits in with your operation.

This is an example only.

Chart "Fifth floor"

This example is for a nursing unit. Cleaning at Level 1, the time needed is 6.43 hours labor time.
This floor has 21 daily patient rooms, and 2 discharge room cleans for this particular day.

B	C Measurments	D	E Sq ft	F How many	G Total sq ft	I # Rooms Today	J Sq ft Today	K Sq ft/ hour	L Hours	M Minutes
						Level		**1**		
Patient Rooms										
Regular rooms - daily cleaning	23	12	276	30	8280	20	5520	1840	3	180
Oversize rooms - daily cleaning			376	1	376	1	376	1840	0.2	12.3
Discharge rooms	23	12	276			2	552	828	0.67	40
Blocks of Nurses stations,	18.6	76	1414	1	1414	1	1414	4200	0.34	20.2
soiled utility, Nurses Locker	18.6	53	986	1	985.8	1	986	4200	0.23	14.1
	18.6	27	502	1	502.2	1	502	4200	0.12	7.17
Corridors - spot dust/wet mop	190	8	1520	2	3040	1	3040			
	20	8	160	4	640	1	640			
Total for Corridors							3680	44160	0.08	5
Waiting room/with restroom	23	12	276	1	276	1	276	1500	0.18	11
Therapy room	32	24	768	1	768	1	768	5000	0.15	9.22
Nurses Break Room	23	12	276	1	276	1	276	1500	0.18	11
Nurses Restroom	8	8	64	1	64	1	64	450	0.14	8.53
Nurses Restroom	8	7	56	1	56	1	56	450	0.12	7.47
45 min lunch, 15 min break = 1 hour									1	
					16678				**6.43** Hours	

Chart "Fifth floor Level 2"

This example is for the same nursing unit, but cleaning at **Level 2** now.
The time needed is 8.72 hours

B	Measurments		Sq ft	How many	Total sq ft	Level 2		2		
						# Rooms Today	Sq ft Today	Sq ft hour	Hours	Minutes
Patient Rooms										
Regular rooms - daily cleaning	23	12	276	30	8280	20	5520	1380	4.00	240.00
Oversize rooms - daily cleaning			376	1	376	1	376	1380	0.27	16.35
Discharge rooms	23	12	276			2	552	662	0.83	50.03
Blocks of Nurses stations, soiled utility, Nurses Locker										
	18.6	76	1414	1	1414	1	1414	2500	0.57	33.93
	18.6	53	986	1	985.8	1	986	2500	0.39	23.66
	18.6	27	502	1	502.2	1	502	2500	0.20	12.05
Corridors - spot dust/wet mop										
	190	8	1520	2	3040	1	3040			
	20	8	160	4	640	1	640			
Total for Corridors							3680	22080	0.17	10.00
Waiting room/with restroom	23	12	276	1	276	1	276	900	0.31	18.40
Therapy room	32	24	768	1	768	1	768	3200	0.24	14.40
Nurses Break Room	23	12	276	1	276	1	276	900	0.31	18.40
Nurses Restroom	8	8	64	1	64	1	64	280	0.23	13.71
Nurses Restroom	8	7	56	1	56	1	56	280	0.20	12.00
45 min lunch, 15 min break = 1 hour									1.00	
					16678				**8.72**	Hours

Chart "Fifth floor Level 3"

This example is for the same nursing unit, but cleaning at **Level 3.**
The time needed is 10.47 hours

B	C	D	E	F	G	I	J	K	L	M
						Level 3				
	Measurements		Sq ft	How many	Total sq ft	# Rooms Today	Sq ft Today	Sq ft hour	Hours	Minutes
Patient Rooms										
Regular rooms - daily cleaning	23	12	276	30	8280	20	5520	1150	4.80	288.00
Oversize rooms - daily cleaning		12	376	1	376	1	376	1150	0.33	19.62
Discharge rooms	23	12	276			2	552	552	1.00	60.00
Blocks of Nurses stations, soiled utility, Nurses Locker										
	18.6	76	1414	1	1414	1	1414	1900	0.74	44.64
	18.6	53	986	1	985.8	1	986	1900	0.52	31.13
	18.6	27	502	1	502.2	1	502	1900	0.26	15.86
Corridors - spot dust/wet mop	190	8	1520	2	3040	1	3040			
	20	8	160	4	640	1	640			
Total for Corridors							3680	14720	0.25	15.00
Waiting room/with restroom	23	12	276	1	276	1	276	692	0.40	23.93
Therapy room	32	24	768	1	768	1	768	2650	0.29	17.39
Nurses Break Room	23	12	276	1	276	1	276	692	0.40	23.93
Nurses Restroom	8	8	64	1	64	1	64	250	0.26	15.36
Nurses Restroom	8	7	56	1	56	1	56	250	0.22	13.44
45 min lunch, 15 min break = 1 hour									1.00	
					16678				10.47	Hours

Chart "Fifth floor Level 4"

This example is for the same nursing unit, but cleaning at **Level 4.**
The time needed is 12.68 hours

B	C	D	E	F	G	I	J	K	L	M
	Measurements		Sq ft	How many	Total sq ft	# Rooms Today	Sq ft/ Today	Sq ft hour	Hours	Minutes
						Level 4				
Patient Rooms										
Regular rooms - daily cleaning	23	12	276	30	8280	20	5520	920	6.00	360.00
Oversize rooms - daily cleaning			376	1	376	1	376	920	0.41	24.52
Discharge rooms	23	12	276			2	552	473	1.17	70.02
Blocks of Nurses stations, soiled utility, Nurses Locker										
	18.6	76	1414	1	1414	1	1414	1650	0.86	51.40
	18.6	53	986	1	985.8	1	986	1650	0.60	35.85
	18.6	27	502	1	502.2	1	502	1650	0.30	18.26
Corridors - spot dust/wet mop										
	190	8	1520	2	3040	1	3040			
	20	8	160	4	640	1	640			
Total for Corridors							3680	11040	0.33	20.00
Waiting room/with restroom	23	12	276	1	276	1	276	562	0.49	29.47
Therapy room	32	24	768	1	768	1	768	2200	0.35	20.95
Nurses Break Room	23	12	276	1	276	1	276	562	0.49	29.47
Nurses Restroom	8	8	64	1	64	1	64	177	0.36	21.69
Nurses Restroom	8	7	56	1	56	1	56	177	0.32	18.98
45 min lunch, 15 min break = 1 hour									1.00	
					16678				**12.68** Hours	

To reach higher levels of cleanliness, will it really take that many more hours?

Probably.

But it's up to you and your crew.

As mentioned, there are not many Michael Phelps around in top physical peak, including this author.

Not many Jim Thorpe's, Roger Bannister's, etc.

And even if there are these miraculous people around, they can't just go leaping about the corridor and running through doorways.

The above charted tasks are performed on a busy nursing unit.

Moving too fast can be a concern of safety.

Running over nurses and patients is not cool, and hurriedly slopping a wet mop over a floor could be a recipe for disaster.

Safety is number one.

But they can motivate themselves to perform higher, it may not be an Olympic Gold Medal, but could be a gold medal for them in heaven – working hard to provide a sparkling clean room for sick people.

The next two charts are from a Cath Lab, shown at Level 1 and 2 only.

Chart "Cath Lab"

This is a Cath Lab, cleaned at Level 1. Labor time needed is 2.99 hours

B	C	D	E	F	G	I	J	K	L	M
						Level		**1**		
		Measurments	Sq ft	How many	Total sq ft	# Rooms Today	Sq ft/ Today	Sq ft hour	Hours	Minutes
Cath Lab										
Cath Lab & control rooms 3 each	61	31	1891	1	1891	1	1891	828	2.28	137.03
Equipment room	35	5	175	1	175	1	175	4200	0.04	2.50
Offices	20	8	160	1	160	1	160	4500	0.04	2.13
Storage	23	12	276	1	276	1	276	19500	0.01	0.85
EVS closet	8	5	40	1	40	1	40	300	0.13	8.00
Corridors, inside - total dust/wet mop										
Corridors	63	8	504	1	504	1	504			
Corridor - inside	21	5	105	1	105	1	105			
Corridor - inside	25	9	225	1	225	1	225			
Total for corridors						1	834	2100	0.40	23.83
Scrub sink area	4	3	12	2	24	1	24	828	0.03	1.74
Frozen room - outside hallway	14	10	140	1	140	1	140	2365	0.06	3.55
					3540				**2.99**	**Hours**

Chart "Cath Lab Level 2"

This is the Cath Lab cleaned at **Level 2**. Labor time needed is 3.89 hours.

B	C	D	E	F	G	I	J	K	L	M
						Level		**2**		
	Measurements		Sq ft	How many	Total sq ft	# Rooms Today	Sq ft/ Today	Sq ft hour	Hours	Minutes
Cath Lab										
Cath Lab & control rooms 3 each	61	31	1891	1	1891	1	1891	662	2.86	171.39
Equipment room	35	5	175	1	175	1	175	2500	0.07	4.20
Offices	20	8	160	1	160	1	160	1000	0.16	9.60
Storage	23	12	276	1	276	1	276	11520	0.02	1.44
EVS closet	8	5	40	1	40	1	40	200	0.20	12.00
Corridors, inside - total dust/wet mop										
Corridors	63	8	504	1	504	1	504			
Corridor - inside	21	5	105	1	105	1	105			
Corridor - inside	25	9	225	1	225	1	225			
Total for corridors						1	834	1830	0.46	27.34
Scrub sink area	4	3	12	2	24	1	24	662	0.04	2.18
Frozen room - outside hallway	14	10	140	1	140	1	140	1656	0.08	5.07
					3540				3.89	Hours

The next four charts are for floor care.

Floor care is certainly at different levels also, because of the different qualities of the work, work practices, and available resources to accomplish the task.

Chart "Floor Crew per year Level 1"

Floor Crew per Year: strip floors, apply 5 coats finish					Level 1			
Sq ft						Sq ft Today	Sq ft hour	Hours	Minutes
		% that needs to be stripped /waxed every 6 months	Total sq ft complete	# of days to					
220266		0.5	110133	260		424	100	4.24	254
		% once a year							
220266		1	220266	260		847	100	8.47	508
								2	
45 min lunch, 15 min break = 1 hour								**14.71**	Hours

Chart "Floor Crew per year Level 2"

Level 2

Floor Crew per Year: strip floors, apply 5 coats finish

Sq ft	% that needs to be stripped /waxed every 6 months	Total sq ft	# of days to complete	Sq ft Today	Sq ft hour	Hours	Minutes
220266	0.5	110133	260				
	% once a year			424	70	6.05	363
220266	1	220266	260	847	70	12.10	726
						2	
						20.15 Hours	

45 min lunch, **15 min break = 1 hour**

Chart "Patient Rooms Spray Buff Level 1"

Patient rooms that need spray buff / once per week, dust before & after, move furniture

Level 1

	Sq ft	Sq ft/ Today	Sq ft/ hour	Hours	Minutes
5th floor	8656	8656	1840	4.70	282.26
4th floor	9860	9860	1840	5.36	321.52
3rd floor - totals	15626	15626	1840	8.49	509.54
2nd floor - totals	16611	16611	1840	9.03	541.66
Totals for floors				27.58	1654.99
			div/ 5 days	**5.52** Hours	

Chart "Patient Rooms Spray Buff Level 2"

Patient rooms that need spray buff / once per week, dust before & after, move furniture

Level 2

	Sq ft	Sq ft/ Today	Sq ft/ hour	Hours	Minutes
5th floor	8656	8656	1380	6.27	376.35
4th floor	9860	9860	1380	7.14	428.70
3rd floor - totals	15626	15626	1380	11.32	679.39
2nd floor - totals	16611	16611	1380	12.04	722.22
Totals for floors				36.78	2206.65
			div/ 5 days	**7.36**	Hours

These are averages for this task.

I've found that to actually clean up correctly after buffing, these numbers are higher.

125. Sq ft per hour on your calculator, plus a question

On calculator,

Total sq ft - divided by - minutes required X 60 minutes = sq ft per hour.

So if I'm cleaning at Level 1, am I cleaning like a Horse Stable?

Perhaps.

The question I ask myself is this:

Do I have supersonic high patient satisfaction scores?

If not, the answer to the above question could be yes.

126. 2 Things

So there are two things going on here.

First, I have a Level 2 saying that I am cleaning at Gas Station cleanliness, and a labor hour number, which is a fixed number that must be met?

No.

I determine what Level of cleanliness and start there.

The labor hour number is a goal to work for, and is an average speed for an average worker.

The number *may* improve (labor hours going down) with better performance from the worker.

Only a few charts were done here, but I hope it helps you in your quest to figure the unique needs of your facility.

127. Festering Over Complicated Numbers

You have to lighten up, dumb it down, so the figures are simple for a starting point.

For a dining room 10' x 20', with hard flooring – how long would it take to sweep/mop that?

This is not a trivial question. Figuring the answer correct is the first step toward putting together a five hundred line or thousand line spreadsheet that absolutely conquers, within a reasonable margin, the number of FTE's you need in the Environmental Services Department.

Uncle Fester say's, "well Earnie, by the time I got my shoes on, fed the dog, turned on the TV for

Alfred's weather forecast, called Bessie to get her recipe to cook up a pot of beans, I guess I could sweep/mop the dinin' room, and it might take ten minutes.

We need a better answer than Uncle Fester's quoted above.

But if you were to measure Uncle Fester's timing for a week, and every day it takes him exactly 10 minutes to mop the dining room – this is his average standard time.

An average standard time for a worker moving at an average speed is a good place to take note as your Minutes to Clean, and this becomes your Level.

What I had done at my hospital, was to start at Level 2, because that is exactly where we were in terms of cleanliness *in the least clean areas*, none of which were patient areas.

We were at a different Level in terms of labor.

You could have a high performance staff, and operate at Level 1.5 in labor, but bring in a 2.3 in terms of cleanliness.

But if I spend more labor time at Level 3, will my building really be more clean?

If the labor time is productive, real cleaning, the answer is yes.

More scrubbing, more wiping, more dusting, more checking, looking, following up; equals less dust, dirt, debris, trash, and unsightly areas.

Remember, to the managers playing with hundreds of thousands of dollars in payroll, the right math may mean the difference in a successful outcome.

In the book of Proverbs, it says the fear of the Lord is the beginning of wisdom.

In housekeeping, the fear that customers may think your building is dirty, is the beginning of understanding.

Math is simple, but it has to be correct, and communicated clearly.

Start with averages.

128. Misc Is Not TIFF

Ok.

So we have the time needed for a task – even have the lunch figured in.

What about the rest of the story.

You could call it miscellaneous, or incidental time.

The time it takes to set up/break down a housekeeping cart.

This time is not thrown in for free (TIFF) as I call it, it's often overlooked, and can be a huge blunder if not placed into calculations.

All time must be accounted for.

129. The Travel Channel? Not TIFF, either

Travelling may be the most overlooked item when figuring cleaning times.

One housekeeper may be responsible for an entire floor or even multiple floors.

Housekeeping supervisors must travel to all areas of the hospital.

Travel time is not something that is normally thought of as a cost.

In the case of a bus travelling down a road; the travel time of the bus must be figured in as a cost, because a bus cannot instantly transport itself from location to location.

In the same way, a housekeeper spends much of her time travelling to cover a physical area. To ignore this time is similar to ignoring the bus time also.

For a total picture, estimates cannot pay attention only to the task time, but also must pay attention to the travel time to get to the task.

Perhaps It's difficult to work on these estimates.

Do the difficult.

130. Excuse Me...

"Please forward my phone calls about a mile down the road", said the cartoon.

Interruptions; where would we be without them?

Somebody needs paper towels; bath tissue; a person needs assistance; a glass vase just busted; someone wants to report finding a carpenter ant on the carpet; a person lost their hat last week – have you found it?

Nobody likes interruptions – they can feel like police interrogations after a couple years of them.

Take a vacation, look at them as a service opportunity, and with that, have a more positive outlook.

We must mention them here, because they are also overlooked in estimated cleaning times.

A hospital housekeeper may be interrupted many times during a day, pulled away from tasks.

If the interruptions happen, it's okay – without them, we have no patients, no customers, no business.

We must mention them here, because a housekeeper is tasked out by the square foot, or number of patient rooms, or both. The ratio of housekeepers per square foot is leveraged out for maximum return.

Scrutinizing the time of a worker in this manner must take into account all the time spent in a shift.

Nothing is TIFF.

Managers sit down and have numbers in front of them, and are expected to hit these production numbers.

I suggest figuring in a minimum of 10 minutes interruption time per 8 hour shift for a housekeeper, and can be as high as 30 minutes.

'May I help you' service is part of the deal.

131. Other Time To Figure

A whole host of things must be in a spreadsheet to cover time.

All the floor care, porters, entryways, stairways, management staff, project workers.

Projects can take up immense time.

Many things not in normal housekeeping will need to be cleaned periodically, and all this is not TIFF.

Things like chairs. There can be hundreds of chairs in a hospital.

Many of them have regular fabric coverings, making them very time consuming to clean. I've found that the time required to clean chairs is so great that, mostly it may not be done depending on staffing, and the chair is simply replaced after years of service.

Buy furniture with easily cleaned surfaces.

Other projects are things like walls, ceilings, doors, plumbing pipes, corners, lighting fixtures, behind furniture and refrigerators, moving furniture, cleaning up behind construction workers, glass windows, cleaning tape goo off surfaces, elevator cleaning.

All kinds of stuff.

132. Factory Work

Assembly lines improve production.

Team cleaning is a form of the factory assembly line.

If team cleaning is not possible at your location, use the assembly line for your project worker.

Five hours of cleaning a single item, moving from room to room.

Scrubbing toilet plumbing and nothing else, for example.

The less a worker has to change equipment or change project assignments in the middle of a shift, the more production.

Focus, always

EXCEPTIONS TO THE RULES

The way to success is through experience, and most of that comes through failure.

– MARK TWAIN

133. Metrics of Speed

Quickness is an absolute, and quality is also.

As hospitals invest more in IT, they need to look at providing EVS with Spectralink or other smart phones for housekeepers, especially in the larger hospitals.

Quick communication means EVS supervisors are not bogged down looking for people.

134. Actual Hallway Mileage May Vary

Many hospitals have travelling beds and furniture. The beds go to surgery, then back up – maybe even to a different room.

Patients are transferred from one room to another on a bed.

Beds are switched, everything is switched.

Furniture may go along with patient. Chairs, over bed tables, etc.

The point is this – it's yet another cost that is almost impossible to place a figure on it. Re-setting up rooms, re-cleaning beds is all part of doing business.

These things have to be done correctly, and there is a cost of labor that should have a calculation.

135. Weekend Business

"Looks like they're open for business"

Soldier talking to another soldier, one minute before hitting the beach of a war zone.

If you work a shift at a hospital on a weekend, you will notice something.

Some of the offices are closed, but the work goes on 24/7.

A tremendous number of people come through a hospital on weekends.

On Saturday's, I used to feel like I was in Vegas; lots of people, and the lights never go off at night – in many areas at least, and you may not can tell the night from day unless you go outside.

Saturdays can be super short staffed in housekeeping.

ER is busy; there is a flood of visitors; there are meetings in the classrooms; public restrooms need ultimate attention; linen must be stocked; labor & delivery can be busy anytime.

Saturday can be the busiest day for discharges, and that means more staff is actually needed on Saturday instead of less.

Since many people can only visit your hospital on a weekend, and there are less attendants potentially taking care of these guests; public opinion of your hospital may suffer the most when you are not even at work, or at a time you thought would be safe because the "business of the week" had wrapped up already.

Weekends are key.

136. The Ferrari in the Garage Illustration

This illustration is how, if you place a red Ferrari in your garage, then come back in a month – what has happened. The Ferrari is caked with a film of dust. Nobody went in there. There was no activity, no people. Yet the dust was piling up.

Now, a hospital costs more than a Ferrari.

Including the facility and equipment, a Ferrari would be chump change compared to the dollars in a hospital.

A hospital will accumulate dust even without any patients in the hospital, just as a Ferrari will accumulate dust without anyone in the garage.

Work must be performed to remove the dust, even if nobody was in the building.

Removing dust is one of the most time consuming chores, because it reaches not only a few ledges, but every surface, including floors.

Every horizontal surface has it, plus some vertical surfaces, and everything must be wiped.

Remove the people from the hospital, and housekeeping will still have work piling up by the day.

A few less patients means you still lose – cleaning never stops.

137. Floor Care and a Dodge Viper

Let's say for the sake of conversation, there was a dark blue Dodge Viper for rent.

The Viper was popular, and always rented out week to week.

Many people over months and months, ran up mileage on the car until a problem occurred: The Viper was so popular that the rental company did not reserve down time for maintenance and therefore the car was not cleaned. Soon the tires needed replacing, two dings in the door and a squeaking windshield wiper needed attention.

One customer had even taken a wrong turn and ended up driving the car through an abandoned corn field overrun with four foot high weeds and briars.

In addition, the "dark blue" paint had some hail damage, the carpets were filthy, the entire interior needed a detail, and "frankly", as the last customer who rented the car replied, "there is a bad smell in there".

So now the $180,000 super charged car was not so much a "Viper" as it was a "Diaper".

Customers vowed to never return to the car rental place after the experience of driving a smelly, beat up vehicle.

Floors in a patient room are something like the Viper.

They can make you look like a supercharged contender that means serious business, but if neglected on the maintenance, will shed customers like peeling an ear of corn.

Many times the rooms, like the Viper, are so popular that very little down time is allowed for maintenance.

If the housekeeping department is turned away from performing this maintenance because the room is continually in use, eventually the customers will notice, and notice in a big way.

Allow time for maintenance.

138. "The Searchers" made for a great movie

In the John Wayne movie, two cowboys roam around the barren countryside for years, searching for a child. In the end, they finally find the young girl.

You may have a version of The Searchers going on in your housekeeping department.

If her mop handle is missing, Maria must go on a long search to find it before work can begin.

In many medium to large hospitals, searching for lost equipment/supplies can collectively take from one hour to several hours per shift.

The main reason for this continual fiasco, is that these hospitals may not have housekeeping closets which can be locked up, or closets so small that the cart cannot fit inside.

There are no easy solutions, but it sure makes the day fascinating.

Organize better when possible.

139. Finding The Lost & Found

An area that usually needs some help:

The Lost & Found Department in a hospital.

A movie came out one year named The Money Pit.

In the movie, Tom Hanks pours money into a worthless house that has no hope.

Lost & Found in a hospital could be thought of as The Time Pit.

Much time is poured into taking care of lost items.

In many cases, Lost & Found is handed to housekeeping, and little resources provided to manage the many phone calls and folks dropping by for inquiries.

In one hospital I worked, the Volunteers took it over. They were able to handle it nicely, and took a load of bricks away from us.

Managing the day to day operations of Lost & Found is not a strong point for housekeeping; for one thing, just running housekeeping alone is a daunting task.

But there is something more.

Here is the reality:

A knock comes at the door, and in steps an elegantly dressed woman searching for an expensive missing personal item. The woman is led to the Lost & Found closet, which is unlocked and loaded with items slightly dusty and even downright dirty that appear to her to be items from 40 years ago. The closet is located inside a room used by the floor maintenance personnel. There are machines, floor pads, brooms and mops scattered about. The room needs a good cleaning. There is one mop bucket that was carelessly not emptied by one of the workers on the previous shift, and the water inside the bucket was filthy and smelled.

This is the room to which the elegantly dressed woman was led, this room in a major 500 bed hospital trying to maintain an image in a highly competitive metro area.

Guess as to what her opinion of this hospital may have been after that encounter.

The room should have been kept clean, but it may be wise to review where guests are asked to go to find their personal lost item, which may be an item dear to them.

If you are struggling with Lost & Found, I suggest to just look on the bright side as this is a service opportunity – helping someone agonizing over the loss of something dear to them.

Losses can have a bright side, especially when you find the thing they are looking for.

Make sure your Found items don't lead to a Lost customer.

140. Guys That Check Your Systems

Men may come in a hospital and start going through the building, repairing things.

This is the visiting vendors I'm talking about.

Vendor guys that go through ceilings, that check electrical systems, electrical devices in patient rooms, corridors, anywhere.

They are some of the hardest working bunch you'll see anywhere, but you need to check after they've left an area – the patient is counting on all parties to clean up after repairs.

Ceiling debris, drips of solutions, sheetrock dust from drilled holes.

Often, paper trash, tape, and other debris are left behind.

Vendors are not really trained on keeping rooms or areas sanitary, they are just supposed to take care of their specialty.

These guys actually save our life when we need their service, but there needs to be understandings – try to get an agreement with them.

Lay ground rules for visiting vendors.

141. Travelling Furniture

There is a shortage on furniture.

Someone is sent out to round up what they can find.

They come across a few tables in abandoned offices.

The tables have a quarter inch of dust caked at the bottom.

These are taken straight to a patient room, without any cleaning.

The job was taken care of, but this is something that cannot be done.

Transferred furniture needs wiping with a disinfectant.

ON TRACK, ON THE MOVE

"Even if you're on the right track, you'll get run over if you just sit there"

– WILL ROGERS

"My men don't dig foxholes. Foxholes only slow up an offensive. Keep moving".

– GENERAL GEORGE S. PATTON

142. Move, People

Trying to get people to move – how to make it happen.

Your people feed off your energy – you are the leader.

Physical energy or mental energy – they both work to stimulate everyone and they feed off it.

You have no energy – they may not either.

Show them by example what to do.

Offer energy for breakfast.

143. Sense Of Urgency

The sense of urgency is a well known phrase, but may not get enough attention.

I've offered the Sense Of Urgency Award for people that demonstrate this quality in their work.

People that come in, get a quick start and respond quickly to requests.

Quick response is a rare quality.

144. Savings & Loans Do Not Make Good Examples

Some folks hit the door early - like after a 6 or 7 hour work day.

There is rubber burning to get out of the parking lot.

I can't blame some of them – folks are over-worked as it is.

You need to motivate your staff.

A concert pianist attracting sold out crowds did not get there by practicing bankers hours.

The individual reaching that height did so by practicing perhaps twelve hours a day.

For decades, bank institutions were known to close early and go home.

In recent years we've seen Savings & Loans go down.

Banks failed & needed taxpayer bailouts.

Banks had "bankers hours" and closed early for the day.

No more.

Some are even opening on weekends now.

In short, short working hours do not produce excellence.

They usually produce failure.

Work on it.

145. Flyers Make Good Cheerleaders

The story goes that a hotel manager placed customer satisfaction surveys in the rooms, but was disappointed when the surveys came back all positive. Seems the housekeepers trashed negative comments before the paper reached the manager.

While this story has some humor in it, the manager in question needs to look in the mirror, and ask him/her self why customers would want to write negative comments in the first place.

A good manager gets personally involved in the rooms, and works to reduce complaints before they happen.

The flyers I designed for patient rooms is two fold; offering complimentary items, plus a line at the bottom that says simply: "dear housekeeping manager, there is something

I would like you to know".

The absolutely astoundingly nice comments we've had about the housekeepers are shared to them, and I think brings out a motivation in them that cannot be bought.

We pay attention to the negative, buy why harbor on them.

Give them all the positive you can.

146. Brands

When possible, allow cleaning brands help you to convey the message of clean. Some brands just have the word "clean" in them, such as Clorox or Lysol.

The products with Clorox, Lysol, Mr. Clean on the label help you say to your patients that you are the Hallmark hospital, by caring enough to use the very best.

The associates appreciate brands also.

Allow at least one brand item in your arsenal.

VENDOR RELATIONS

147. Grant Was A Quartermaster

I have read that General Ulysses S. Grant was a quartermaster before he was a general.

By the time he came to head of the ranks, he knew how to get supplies to his men.

The people that supply the troops can make or break you.

I have seen and heard, stories about how a large business decided to give a tiny vendor an order just because they wanted to do it.

I know first hand, because I was one of those vendors many years ago.

I can tell you that, it can be a humbling experience that a customer would want to give you an order even while they could purchase the same thing from their current vendor.

When a tiny business is given a large order by a large company, what is the dynamic that can occur.

Well, you will see the large company offered the lowest possible pricing, and offered the best service in town by that tiny business.

The large company may not have known how big of an impact this order was to this vendor.

It was not the size of the order – it was that the large company could have ordered from an existing vendor.

The only way the tiny business could show how grateful its feelings were toward this large company, was to make the delivery the same day as ordered, and the tiny business sacrificed, and placed all other business dealings aside when this large company even whispered one word toward it.

The large company was not used to this kind of service, and decided to form a long term partner-ship with the tiny business.

Treat vendors well. They might give you hand grenades when you've been fighting a battle with swords.

148. But I Have A Contract

You have a special opportunity every time someone from the local community contacts you to solicit business.

I already may have contracts, but how I respect people in the community can indirectly have a negative or positive effect on a hospital/business depending on the respect I offer them.

Even if there is not much of a chance for a salesperson to make a sale to your facility, giving them a few minutes of your time does no harm. In turn, they may speak highly of you - talk to others in your town about the nice person they encountered at the hospital/business.

Quick meetings to simply be cordial to local people is the right thing to do.

Local salespeople are also local customers.

Treat them well.

Cordiality is the right thing to do.

149. Appreciate em'

Your vendors are your partners.

They are your suppliers.

Makes no difference that they don't work directly for your hospital/company. They work for you indirectly.

Since they work for you, they should not be immune to the same kind of recognition.

A Vendor Appreciation Day may do as much for morale among the vendors as a Hospital Week does for associates.

They are your partners in business.

Behind the scenes, vendors are probably doing more than you ever imagined to get your orders delivered on time.

Your purchasing and materials management personnel are right there with them, delivering on tight schedules, unloading multiple truckloads on blistering hot and freezing cold docks - hand in hand with these vendors to get the job done.

Show them you are aware of their service.

FINAL THOUGHTS

150. Re-Fuel

During the course of the year, you may face budget set-backs.

You may be asked to do with less, but to keep operations going, which may not be pleasant to deal with at that time.

I like to think of the story when General Patton's Third Army ran out of fuel on August 31, 1944, just outside of Metz, France.

"If I just had a few miserable gallons of gasoline, Patton had said,

I could go all the way to Berlin."

Eisenhower may not have been able to give Patton what he needed at the time, but later Patton received his gasoline.

Remember that running out of fuel is not a failure – you are not defeated.

Eventually you should be able to re-fuel, and go on to win the battle.

Use the resources you have to make do.

151. Cliff Young

Australia's 543 mile endurance race is considered one of the most difficult marathons.

In 1983, Cliff Young showed up out of nowhere to start.

He just walked up and said he'd like to enter the race.

This was a race for professional athletes, but they did allow walk-ons.

61 years old, he wore overalls and work boots.

He told his story to the press, who thought he was crazy, about how he grew up on a farm and had to chase sheep.

"I believe I can run this race", he told them.

The professional athletes knew that to be successful, a runner had to run about 18 hours a day for 5 days, and sleep for 6 hours a day.

Cliff did not know what the other athletes were doing, he just knew that he had better do whatever it takes to be competitive.

The professionals were way ahead of Cliff on the first day, but little by little, day by day, Cliff surpassed them to win the race.

He was able to win by not sleeping.

When he was awarded the $10,000 prize, Cliff said he didn't know there was a prize, and gave the money away to other runners.

The moral to this story is – don't listen to professionals about how you are "unable" to compete because of your limitations.

The will to win is about whatever turns you on to get the job done. Money may have nothing to do with it.

It's about you.

152. The Right Stuff

A lottery winner, won the lottery by buying the right ticket at the right time.

Maybe there's some luck there, maybe luck is all it was.

A movie called The Right Stuff highlighted a small part of the career of Chuck Yeager.

Chuck Yeager may have been lucky on some occasions, but mostly it was his passion for his work and his experience that allowed him to be the first man to break the sound barrier.

Can you steer yourself into the right place or right time?

Yeager did not fly the X-1 and break the sound barrier after only a couple test flights.

An ace in WWII with a lengthy career, he flew and tested hundreds of aircraft.

Something else – he was in tune with his aircraft and studied all the mechanics of an aircraft. He could tell the designers and engineers when something was wrong with their design.

He steered himself into the right place by doing what he loved, with a passion.

And he developed the right stuff along the way, all that experience building the character of the man.

The timing of it, though, is not necessarily in the hands of an individual.

The right time for you to shine may reveal itself when you least expect it.

Do your part, God gives final OK.

153. Blundering, Succeeding

Another tidbit from The Searchers – never quit.

Sure, the other guys may be better, have the upper hand.

While quietly, you are learning, reading, listening.

Even if blundering, your goal is making progress.

– *"I was there when the Americans blundered into Berlin in 1917"* – from the movie Casablanca

If you are in chaos, thriving on chaos is possible.

If your world is not perfect, endeavor to survive and organize.

Outlast.

154. For Those That Seek It

"If you look for truthfulness, you might just as well be blind; It always seems to be so hard to give. Honesty is such a lonely word"

– BILLY JOEL

Taking an honest path is not just the best policy, it is the only way for long term success.

Loads of successful people have an honesty about them that comes to the surface and is noticeable – in their face, eyes, and gestures.

In the end, why not feel the satisfaction of knowing that you were tested the other way, but instead kept an honesty about you that others found refreshing.

To go walking in Billy Joel's "River of Dreams",

"searching for something" as his lyrics alluded – and that something he is looking for is probably the truthfulness he sings about in his Honesty song.

You were tempted for sure, but outlasted all obstacles.

Dishonesty was not even considered.

I'll end with a word of encouragement to you.

Overcome the obstacles.

** http://shura.shu.ac.uk/913/1/fulltext.pdf

** www.pickereurope.org

** Swim with the sharks without being eaten alive.

Harvey Mackay

** Marriott.com The Marriott Philosophy

Made in the USA
Las Vegas, NV
06 July 2021

26046532R00125